## ACKNOWLEDG

First, I want to than~ ~, ~ord and Savior, Jesus Christ. He has promised His people:

*"Blessed are ye when men shall revile you and persecute you, and shall say all manner of evil against you falsely for My sake. Rejoice and be exceeding glad, for great is your reward in heaven; for so persecuted they the prophets who were before you." Matthew 5:11-12*

I also thank God for my father, Archbishop Dr. M. A. Thomas. His spiritual life has been an example and an inspiration for me. I want to praise the Lord for my wife, Shelley, who stood by me during this period of crisis. She is a true life-mate worthy of trust and honor. I am grateful to God for my two sons - Steven and Timothy, who continually pray for me.

We were assisted by many during this time of severe persecution. The following advocates presented our side of the matter in the court of law - Dr. Brahm Dutt, Venkatesh, Shard Purohit, R. K. Jain, Vinay Garg, Suraya Kant, Madhav Mitra, and Mohammed Akram.

Others who worked diligently behind the scenes were: Mathew Samuel, Raj Peter, Daisy Paulose, Punnen, Dr. Sajan George, Babu C. J., Dr. John Dayal, Dr. K. P. Yohannan, Dr. A.

F. P., Dr. Abraham Mathai, Dr. John Mathew, Dr. Sam George, Dr. P. G. Varghese, Samuel Abraham, Jacob Mathew, Sajikutty, Hejang, Stephen C., Morrison Baby, Trevor Freeman, Jessy Thomas, James Abraham, Shanti Dhariwal, Salim Bharti, Shaukin, Pankaj Mehta, Omji, Bhusan, Jetha, Vijay Nair, S. D. Paul, Abdul Jajeed, Ramprasad, Vidya Nair, my sisters Elizabeth and Mary, Alice John and Harneet Kaur.

So many loving families of believers – from a variety of Christian denominations – helped us - even visited me while I was in prison. Although I cannot list all of the names here, I do want to especially mention the Senior Pastor of The Pentecostal Mission – Pastor Thomas – who sent money for us during this time of crisis. He also spent many sleepless nights praying for us.

I also want to thank the media for carrying the news of my arrest and imprisonment to the general public which kept the public informed of the latest developments in the case. The reports published by leading newspapers in India helped us greatly.

I also want to thank God for the Honorable Minister Madan Dilawar who used all of his power to test the strength of the foundation upon which Emmanuel Mission International was built; a foundation established by God. Our God sends tests of faith to all of us. In our case, He used the Minister as His testing instrument and we want to thank God for it.

Finally, I can honestly say that I am grateful to the large army of religious fundamentalists whose attacks both tested and strengthened my spiritual life. The Bible tells us,

*"Therefore I take pleasure in infirmities, in reproaches, in necessities, in persecutions, in distresses for Christ's sake: for when I am weak, then am I strong." 2 Corinthians 12:10*

**Dr. Samuel Thomas**

## FOREWORD

I dedicate this book to the memory of my father, Dr. M. A. Thomas (*1935-2010*) and my mother, Ammini Cherian Thomas (*1934-1995*).

My parents taught me and my two sisters to always remain firm in the Christian faith and its teachings. My mother repeatedly told me: "Be faithful unto death, and the crown of life shall be yours." (*Revelations 2:10*)

When I matured into a young man and began to share the responsibilities of the ministry with my father, I began to see God's blessing in great measure. Yet, along with those blessings came much opposition from non-Christians. I would determine – many times as a young man – that I was going to leave Kota. My father would simply ask me, "Can we close down the ministry of God? Was not Jesus also insulted? Did He not face persecution as well? Was not the church built upon the blood of the martyrs?" He would also remind me of the following:

*"Now in fact all who want to live godly lives in Christ Jesus will be persecuted" 2 Tim. 3:12*

Then he would proceed to encourage me with:

*"...being confident of this, He who began a good work in you will carry it on to completion until the day of Christ Jesus." Philippians 1:6*

During the past few years, the anti-Christians have tried to kill me and my father several times. They would attempt to discredit the ministry so that the work would be shut down. On March 3, 2006, an anti-Christian group, the Hindu Raksha Samiti, even went so far as to offer a reward of $55,000 to anyone who would cut off my father's head. At this time, my father was 72 years old.

For over 50 years my father gave his life to serving the needy and destitute. He was even awarded the Padma Shri in recognition of his humanitarian work by the Indian government! The anti-Christians have tried repeatedly to force the government to revoke this tribute. My father's only response was, "I love my India. I love the people of Kota."

I wrote most of this book while in prison. My objective for writing this book is to encourage all Christians to fight the battle of faith and be victorious so that each of our lives will bring glory to the Lord's name. Those of us who were imprisoned feel honored that God would find us worthy of being jailed, because of His Word. We are not ashamed of this (*1 Peter 4:6*). We pray that His name will continuously be glorified at all times through us.

We also recognize that the Gospel is working on the hearts of many people because of what we continue to suffer (*Philippians 1:12*). We are also grateful to all who continue to inquire about the persecution that continues even today (*Philippians.4:14*).

**Dr. Samuel Thomas**

# TABLE OF CONTENTS

*"Blessed are they that are persecuted for righteousness' sake, for theirs is the Kingdom of Heaven." Matthew 5:10*

# Chapter I

## 1960 - The beginning of Hopegivers International

Over 50 years ago my parents - Dr. M. A. Thomas (*1935-2010*) and Ammini Cherian Thomas (*1934 – 1995*) travelled 1500 miles to the city of Kota after graduating from Bible College. They began the ministry with nothing but a desire to serve the oppressed and preach the Gospel.

Although they were Indian, they learned quickly that this part of India – in which they felt called to minister in 1959 - didn't want any part of Christianity or Christians. Initially, its culture, traditions and language were a challenge for my parents. Because they were open about their Christianity, no one wanted to rent them a house. They were very poor, so all they could afford was a motor garage with no windows, electricity or indoor plumbing. They spent the first four years of their ministry in this garage, and experienced first hand, the severe heat of summers and the extreme cold winters. Yet their two daughters – my sisters - were born during the time they were living in this garage.

Although I am writing about the persecution we have been suffering primarily since 2006, it is important that our readers know that persecution has always been a part of this ministry. Over these past 50 years, my father has been thrown into prison and beaten numerous times by anti-Christians.

Beatings, insult, scorn and poverty have been my parents constant companions.

Dad decided to establish a name for the ministry. They named it Emmanuel Society, because it means "God with us". Originally, the ministry consisted of a small church. Their desire to help the destitute of the community and its surrounding villages led to the development of other ministries under the banner of Emmanuel Society. The ministry is now known world wide as Hopegivers International. We have a home office in Kota and one in the United States.

Through much prayer and fasting, God continues to move in the hearts of people all over the world to help us financially build schools, Bible Colleges, and orphanages so we can rescue the abandoned and at-risk children all over India and around the world. We have built one hospital and a Para-medical Clinic - where our nurses are trained. We have many thousands of churches. These beginnings all took place in the wastelands of Rajasthan, due only to the awesome and abundant grace of God. Hopegivers International has established the following ministries in India and other parts of the world (*as of 2011*):

**Churches ................over 43,000 established since 1973**

**Orphanages ..............108 since 1978**

**Schools ...................86 since 1967**

**Bible Colleges .............1**

**Bible Institute .............103**

**Hospital ..................1**

**Para-Medical Institute ......1**

The journey you are about to take with me - as I share my experiences of 2006–2007 - came about as a result of the many successes Hopegivers International experiences in ministry. This success continues to be a painful irritation to anti-Christians throughout India. They have done their best to stop the growth of the church. They have accused us of being traitors, spies, and even terrorists. Although unfounded, their constant accusations have created hatred for us in the hearts of many communities in India. They use social pressure, political coercion, and intimidation wherever possible in order to terrorize us so we will leave Kota and abandon the children. They have only one objective - to wipe out the mission and kill its Founder and Chairman, Dr. M. A. Thomas (1935-2010) and its President, me. All of this hatred and scheming eventually culminated into a warrant for the arrest of my elderly father and me in early 2006.

We have worked hard to put the fires of hatred out in the hearts of these rebels, but have not been successful. We even cancelled our annual Christian Convention in early 2006 in hopes of appeasing the rebels and calming the community. It didn't matter to the rebels that the convention – a graduation ceremony – was held on ministry property. Every year we inform the local police and other city officials of this gathering. We give them plenty of lead time to prepare for the increased influx of visitors to Kota. Believers from within India and many from abroad come to watch as our students receive their degrees from the Bible Institutes, the College and Seminary, and are sent out for their first ministry assignment. The convention was set for February 23-26, 2006 and nearly 10,000 students were scheduled to graduate in Kota.

In spite of our efforts to reduce the tension, year after year we must deal with multiple threats and vandalism from the anti-Christian groups. They will stop at nothing in order to disrupt the convention. But in 2006, the pressure on the local government from the anti-Christian constituency was unusually intense. In the previous three years, local police were comfortable that they could protect the convention participants from these rebels, but not this time. We had to cancel the convention and move it away from Kota.

The anti-Christians had prepared a different plan of attack in 2006 in order to stop God's people. Since intimidation and vandalism had not worked well in the past for them, they decided to use a book entitled, **Haqeeqat** (*Truth or Reality*), to antagonize an already delicate relationship between the Hindu and the Christians in many communities. Most of the villagers would never read the book, so whatever the rebels claimed as truth would likely be believed by the common person. Although the book was among many we have in the Bible Institute Library, we were in no way responsible for writing or publishing the book. We also do not teach the contents of this book. The rebels claim that the book is anti-Hindu. They used the media quite effectively to publicize false information about the content of the book, along with claims that the Thomas' were responsible for writing and publishing the book. Since the majority of people take what the media says at face value, the people in the community believed the false accusations.

The legal case filed against Dad and I accuse us of speaking derogatorily of their Hindu gods and goddesses. If this accusation were to be held up in the courts, Dad and I could be sentenced to three years in prison. This was the basis of the arrest warrant issued for me and my father by the Rajasthan police in February, 2006.

It might help to give you a little history of the book, **Haqeeqat**. It was originally written in English in the 1990's by a Christian lawyer in response to an earlier book entitled, "*A Bunch of Thoughts*". The earlier book was written by the late Guru, M. S. Golwalkar in the 1940's. **Haqeeqat** became controversial when the anti-Christians decided that it was written to refute the assertions made by Guru Golwalkar, who was once the leader of the Rashtriya Swayamsewak Sangh (RSS). The RSS is a Hindu nationalist organization that is active throughout India. Their philosophy demands cultural nationalism from every citizen. Their goal is to preserve the spiritual and cultural traditions of India. Their followers see Hinduism, not simply as a religion, but a way of life. The RSS is viewed as controversial because they resort to violence in order to stop conversions of a Hindu citizen to other religions. Some educators and commentators refer to their tactics as "fascist" in nature.

The book **Haqeeqat** is a Hindi language translation of the original book, which was originally written in English. It simply elaborates the differences between what Scripture says and what the Hindus believe. It does not insult the revered Hindu leader or the Hindu gods and goddesses. In fact, the book was actually widely distributed among government officials in India, including the President, Prime Minister, and the cabinet members when it was originally published in the 1990's. The English version has been available in book stores throughout the country. When I learned that this was the basis of our arrest warrants, I wasn't too concerned about it since I knew we had nothing to do with the book. I was certain that the facts would come out very quickly in court. **I was so wrong.**

A non-bailable warrant was issued to arrest M. G. Mathew, the author of *"Truth or Reality"*, but they could not find him. They fully intended to prosecute him for a criminal offense. Their actions concerning this book are fueled by an unreasonable hatred that makes a mockery of the secular democratic law, and the Constitution of India. After my arrest, the government of Rajasthan banned the book. They also issued arrest warrants for Nathaniel Dennis, the man who translated the book from English into Hindi.

Our ministry has never promoted this book to anyone. It was never distributed or sold to others with the intent of insulting anyone. We never distributed leaflets containing portions of the book - although we were accused of doing so. No statements have ever been made concerning the book or its contents from the podium or using any loud speakers.

The media continued to report the false accusations made by the anti-Christians without ever verifying whether they were valid. Not one media outlet ever printed or even verbalized the sections of the book that were reportedly "provocative" and being used as the legal basis for our arrest warrants. Unfortunately, those who did know the truth remained silent. They were silent because they did not want to be on the receiving end of the violence being promised by the religious fanatics.

By using the media the way they did, the anti-Christians managed to turn other religious groups against us as well. The listening public didn't recognize the conspiratorial intent behind all the false claims. Like many people, if it's on the TV, the radio, or in the newspaper, many think it must be true. I don't really believe that they were worried about their gods and goddesses being insulted. They simply wanted to drive the ministry into oblivion. Even some members of smaller Christian organizations began treating us as if we were enemies. They began to boycott us. Through this experience I learned that sometimes our biggest enemy in Christian work is other Christians who don't want to see the other ministries grow. It is a device used by the devil to promote disunity among believers so the Gospel will be hindered. The whole city was caught up in the grip of this lie. Others did remain friendly and prayed for us, but they kept silent, because they feared for their own lives. Many of our employees quit their jobs and left Kota all together.

The majority of Hindus are tolerant and peace loving people. It is a small, organized, and powerful group within the Hindu community that is not that way. They are the ones who have led the persecution.

Although I knew the political situation had been heating up for several months prior to my trip to the states in 2006, it wasn't until Dad and I were at the airport in Atlanta – bags checked - that we received a call concerning the gravity of the situation. That is when we learned that the Kota police had arrested some of the men who work for the ministry and had detained many others for questioning. I remember - as if it were yesterday - Dad turning to me and asking, "What do you want to do?" If I went back to India, it was certain that we would be in the midst of severe persecution and possibly even killed. Yet there was no discussion between us. We both knew what God would have me do. We simply began to pray as we waited for the flight that would separate me from my family for 14 very long and difficult months.

> *"'For my thoughts are not your thoughts, neither are your ways my ways,' declares the Lord." Isaiah 55:8*

When we arrived in India, I went to Kerala to officiate at a graduation and Dad went to Andhra Pradesh to officiate at another. Because I knew of the arrest warrants issued for both of us, I asked Dad to stay in Andhra Pradesh until I could get things straightened out legally. By this time they had already arrested Mr. R. S. Nair, Emmanuel's Administrator, Mr. V. S. Thomas, Director of the Kota Orphanage, and the young Bible student who was in charge of the bookstall when the undercover officer purchased the book at our convention in October, 2005. Mr. Nair and his wife were very upset about his arrest since they were not even Christians.

When Mr. Nair retired at age 58 from the railroad, he asked if he could work for the ministry as its administrator. He was very good at his job.

Unfortunately, although he heard the Gospel message many times, he and his wife never came to Christ.

But let's start at the beginning – **March 17, 2006**!

*"He makes me lie down in green pastures; he leads me beside quiet waters…Psalm 23:2*

# CHAPTER 2

## Samuel: The First Day, March 17, 2006

I was in Noida, a suburb of Delhi on March 17, 2006. I had just finished speaking at a large graduation ceremony in Kerala. I did not go directly back to Kota because I would have been arrested before I had an opportunity to get some legal advice. Because of my decision not to return directly back to Kota, I did have some accusers who claimed I was fleeing persecution, but they were wrong. If that were true, I would not have left my family and the safety of the United States on February 14. I would not have returned repeatedly to India after the threats on my life began in 1992! I was in Noida to secure bail for the three staff members who had already been arrested, and to apply for preliminary bail for Dad and me. The preliminary bail would keep us out of jail. I also wanted to make sure that everything concerning the orphans was legally in place to protect them should I get arrested. Remember, even the Apostle Paul left certain areas in order to avoid attacks. *Acts 17:5-10; 17: 13-14*

Arriving from Kerala, I met with three friends, Dr. Sajan George, President of Global Christian Council; Dr. Brahm Dutt, President of India's Leper Association; and the Pastor of our orphanage in Delhi. They offered to accompany me to Noida as I sought legal counsel.

Traveling by jeep, we arrived in time for our noon appointment with Mr. R. K. Jain, a senior lawyer for the Supreme Court.

Just as we entered the gates to the courtyard of Mr. Jain's office, thirteen plain clothed men grabbed me from behind and put a revolver to my head announcing, "You are under arrest!" Since none of them were in uniform, we didn't have any idea who was arresting me. By law, police from other states are to be accompanied by local uniformed police in order to make an arrest when they are out of their own territory.

Within seconds of grabbing me, the man holding the gun to my head pulled the trigger. It did not go off! I learned later that these men had hoped I would struggle so they could kill me in the encounter. They really didn't want to have the hassle of an arrest and the travel it required to take me back to Kota. I remember him cussing when the gun misfired. You see, there was a $73,000 reward on my head. I guess he thought I would be less trouble if I was dead and he could still collect the bounty. Clearly, God had other plans!

Once they had me handcuffed, he didn't dare pull the trigger again. There were several lawyers standing around in the courtyard where they had just grabbed me. A second shot would have been seen as a clear case of murder. One of my friends spoke up and asked if they had a warrant to arrest me. One officer's response was, "My gun is my warrant!"

I can't even begin to tell you how helpless and confused I felt in those first few moments. Everything happened so fast. We were totally taken off guard. I thought I was safe as long as I wasn't in Kota, but clearly the enemy was taking no chances. After the initial shock, the words from *Luke 12:7* came to mind:

> *"Indeed, the very hairs of your head are all*
> *numbered. Don't be afraid;*
> *you are worth more than many sparrows."*

I was immediately comforted, knowing that nothing would happen to me unless it was God's will. The Lord was watching everything that was going on. The plain clothed men did finally identify themselves as Rajasthan police to both me and the others in the courtyard. Evidently, someone leaked my location to them. They had rented a vehicle and they drove to Noida to await my arrival.

When you rent a vehicle in India, it automatically comes with a driver. When the poor driver of this rental vehicle saw what was happening to me, he became so terrified that he couldn't drive. Evidently none of the officers from Rajasthan could drive either. All 13 of them stuffed themselves into the jeep and forced me to drive them to the nearest train station.

When we arrived at the Delhi Railway Station, they took all of my personal belongings – wrist watch, belt, wallet, pen and shoe strings. Have you ever tried walking in your shoes when the shoe strings have been removed? They discovered that they didn't have enough money between them to buy train tickets for all of us, so they helped themselves to my wallet. They wanted to buy tickets for the air conditioned car, but decided against it. They bought the open air car tickets instead. March through June is the hottest season of the year in India. Temperatures can range from 90 to 120 degrees in the shade. We all crammed ourselves, like cattle, into an already crowded open air car and began a several hour journey that would take me to the Kota jail.

*"They urgently requested Festus, as a favor to them, to have Paul transferred to Jerusalem, for they were preparing an ambush to kill him along the way." Acts 25:3*

During the train ride, the police badgered me with the same questions over and over again. Periodically, they would slip in an outrageous statement like, "We know that you have declared a reward of 10 million Rupees for the head of Mr. Madan Dilawar, the Social Welfare Minister of the Rajasthan Government. We know that this threat is in retaliation for his promise to pay 1.1 million Rupees to whoever will cut off the head of your father, Dr. M. A. Thomas." I answered calmly, but firmly. "We are followers of the truth. We are commanded to forgive. We pray for the long life of this minister, and we pray for everyone in the Indian Administration starting with the President and the Prime Minister along with the staff in every department. The Bible commands us to do so;

*"...requests, prayers, intercessions, and thanksgiving be made for everyone, for kings and for all those in authority, that we may lead peaceful and quiet lives in all godliness and holiness."*
*1Timothy 2:2*

They asked me if I knew my father's cell phone number. Of course, my Dad was in hiding at that point, but I honestly didn't remember the number. We had gone through 68 cell phones in less than a month. I still had all the papers on me that we were taking to the lawyer when they arrested me; so they took all of those documents from me.

As we reached Sawai Madhopur, the first train stop after leaving New Delhi, an already bad situation turned worse for everyone on the train. A mob made up of hundreds of religious fanatics had gathered at the stop and clearly planned to viciously attack the train. They had no concern for all the innocent people who could be injured because of their hatred for me. The danger of the situation traveled quickly throughout the train. Passengers and even bystanders at the station were terrified. Even the police feared for their own lives as they watched the out of control rage of this mob build minute by minute. They were screaming over and over again, "Bring Samuel Thomas out of the train. We want to kill him." They began to throw rocks at the train, breaking windows out of the air conditioned compartments. I guess they assumed that's where the police were holding me. We saw others with cans of gasoline who clearly intended to set the train on fire if the police didn't hand me over to them. But they didn't get their way, because our God is a faithful God. Not one pebble hit me. When the police holding me saw that the situation was spiraling out of control, they immediately ordered the train to depart.

The police tried to convince me to close the orphanages and stop preaching. They told me that if I would agree to do that, they could let me go. That's when I realized that the accusations concerning the book **Haqeeqat** were just a ruse. What the authorities really want from us is the collapse of our God-ordained mission – the rescue of abandoned and at-risk children. To this day, it isn't the terror of those moments that remain vivid for me. It was the unexplainable peace of that moment which changed my life forever. In those moments of apparent chaos, on March 17, 2006, the Holy Spirit spoke to my heart and assured me that I was right where God wanted me.

I was told later that one of our pastors and his wife – both had grown up in the Kota orphanage - were near enough to observe the mobs screaming for my blood, and throwing rocks at the train in an attempt to kill me. He told me that he could only watch and weep. He prayed that the God we both loved and lived for would protect me.

Clearly the news of my arrest had spread quickly. From the size of that mob, the public must have learned of my arrest prior to us even boarding the train in Delhi. We don't know who leaked the information, but it must have been someone who favored the anti-Christian point of view. The mob wasn't composed of the general public either. It was composed of the religious fanatics who are seriously anti-Christian and bent on violence. They fully intended to take the law into their own hands.

As the train began to slow down just outside of the Kota City limits, every police cell phone rang. I later learned that Dr. Sajan George, Mr. Braham Dutt and others went to the National Human Rights Commission to ask for an order of protection, fearing my death. Due to their urgent requests to intervene for my safety, police superiors were letting the men who held me know that a huge mob numbering over 7000 was waiting for us at the Kota train stop. The mob was out for blood - mine. They were all armed with swords, rocks and gasoline. When I learned of the situation, I couldn't help but be a little amused. After all, just how many Indians does it take to kill one man? With a smile on my face, I found myself thanking the Lord for inserting a little humor in the midst of this chaos.

I am so grateful that the police proceeded in a professional manner. I found myself silently repeating, *Luke 8:50,*

*"...fear not; believe only..."*

Once the train stopped, prior to crossing the river into Kota which was far enough away so the mob couldn't get to me quickly, 150 armed guards from the Reserve Armed Forces took me into protective custody. Seeing the large gathering of armed guards, the few anti-Christians who were waiting for my arrival at this stop, began screaming "This is Samuel Thomas. Finish him off." Before this crowd – now working itself into a frenzy – could attack the police, they got me safely into one of the police stations at the edge of town. By this time it was 7pm on March 17th.

Shortly after my arrival, the police received secret information that insurgents were planning to attack the police station. That's when they immediately transferred me to a larger police station and put me into detention. Once in detention, the relentless questioning began again and continued without a break until 3:00 am. I was interrogated by officials at every level. By this time, I was exhausted, defeated, and broken. The continuous grilling had shaken me, and they would not allow me to sleep. My life's verse has always been, *Philippians 3:10.*

*"I want to know Christ and the power of His resurrection and the fellowship*

*of sharing in His sufferings, becoming like Him in His death…"*

On March 17, 2006, I found myself standing in the very center of that answered prayer!

# CHAPTER 3

### Shelley (*Samuel's wife*): Learns of Samuel's arrest

I did not learn of Samuel's arrest for several hours after he was taken. You see, when it is night here in the states, it is day in India. And then, of course, my computer was downstairs. By the time I checked my emails early the next morning, it had already been four hours since Samuel had been taken into custody. The pastor who emailed me initially could not tell me who arrested Samuel, or where they were taking him. I think that was the most frightening part of those first few hours.

I remember the horrible sinking feeling I had in my stomach as I read that first email. I could barely breathe. At this point, I didn't know if he was dead or alive. It was another six hours before I knew he was still alive, although in serious physical danger. It was the Delhi pastor who called and let me know where he had been taken. Surprisingly – even to me - I didn't fall apart that first day. My mind began clattering immediately about all the possible options and the people who could help us keep Samuel safe. I called my parents right away and asked if they could come to Georgia and stay with the boys while I made arrangements to leave for Washington D.C. the next day. I knew it would be critical that I put a face on Samuel and Hopegivers International for anyone who might have the power to help him.

The Executive Director from Hopegivers International accompanied me to DC where we met with anyone who might be able to positively impact Samuel's situation. We met with assistants to the Congressmen, if we couldn't personally meet with the Congressmen. We met with the people at the State Department who make religious freedom and the violations of that freedom a priority.

It turned out that McLean Bible Church in Virginia, which sends mission teams out every year, became a real blessing for us. Scott and Susan Sweat had just returned in January of 2006 from a trip to India where they had met Papa (*M. A. Thomas*) and Samuel. This couple and their church were instrumental in having a letter drawn up by Roger Wicker, who was a Mississippi Congressman in 2006, but is now a Senator. The document was co-sponsored by W. Todd Akin, the Congressman from MO. The letter firmly suggested that Samuel Thomas was to be treated fairly. This letter contained a total of 22 signatures – all of them U. S. Congressmen who were interested in Samuel's welfare. That document was submitted immediately to the Indian government.

The letter was circulated among President Bush's inner circle of friends, although nothing was made official at that time. Still, it must have been spoken of privately with some powerful people, because once the letter's content was circulated to India's political officials, they communicated immediately with the officials at the local jail where Samuel was being held. His treatment by the police took a turn for the better, although by this time, it was weeks after he had been arrested. That letter motivated them to move him from isolation in a rat infested 3'x 5' cell – where he was in solitary confinement - to the cell where his colleagues were being held.

The Commission for Human Rights in Delhi was literally overwhelmed with pleas for Samuel's safety through faxes and emails. Christians – both American and Indian alike - continued to bombard them. I didn't attempt to go to India after Samuel's arrest; I knew that my presence would only complicate things for him. My responsibility continued to be the care of our boys and making an attempt at creating a somewhat normal life for them.

When I told the boys – without going into great detail – of their Dad's arrest, they were obviously concerned. But I had to smile at my oldest son's response when I told them of the arrest. Steven said, "Boy, when Dad gets out of this one, he will have more good stories to tell." Steven had become used to hearing about death threats over the years, but he was confident that his Dad would ultimately be released.

Although I didn't share my concerns with the boys, I was more troubled this time than at any other time we had endured persecution. In the past, the accusations came from individuals or some radical cell. This time the government was involved in trying to get rid of Samuel. We were put in the position of being assumed guilty until we could prove we were innocent. To this day, they continue to keep us in legal limbo – just because they can!

Soon after Samuel was arrested, I asked the US staff to shut down the Hopegivers International web page. I couldn't take the chance that someone in India would go in to the site and twist something that was written on it so they could keep Samuel in jail even longer. It can sometimes be the most innocently placed phrase that could be used to incriminate Samuel even further.

Because the local police who were escorting Samuel every couple of days between the jail and the court house didn't personally have a gripe against Samuel, they would allow his friends to walk alongside him and visit. Once in a while – always being very discreet - Samuel would ask them to send me a message from one of their blackberries and reassure me that he was okay. One of his messages read, "I'm proud of you; I love you."

After Samuel was arrested that March, I would find some comfort by listening to a lot of Christian praise music. There were times when I would let it play all night long. My prayer life at that time? Honestly, sometimes I just didn't have words – only tears. A friend of mine gave me a CD that repeated the names of the Lord and their meanings. That CD became a transfusion of comfort which strengthened my soul during those days. Even so, I must tell you that living on the edge of your seat takes a lot out of you!

I guess I always knew this day could come. Samuel had already escaped death many times in the past. After all, we are Christians making a major impact for the Kingdom of God in India. It only stands to reason that the enemy would want to remove us from harvesting the fields for the Father.

I remember Christmas Eve in 2005. We had travelled separately to the orphanage located at the edge of Kota for their Christmas program. Samuel and his driver remember hearing what sounded like a backfire. Some time later, a man was admitted to the hospital with injuries to his face from a gun that had misfired. When questioned, he admitted that he had been hired to kill Samuel. It was a homemade gun and clearly not well made – by God's grace!

In the past, police have found bombs planted at events where Samuel was scheduled to speak. Once when Samuel had to cancel a speech at the last minute, he unknowingly thwarted another assassination attempt. It seems that the hotel room that had been reserved for him remained unoccupied after the cancellation. But people on the same floor as the reserved hotel room kept hearing a ruckus coming from the room. When hotel security checked it out, they found two men dressed in black with knives. When Samuel didn't show up for his own execution, they decided to get drunk and enjoy the benefits of a free room.

When an undercover person attended one of the extremists meetings in 2001, he learned of a plot to kidnap our two boys. Their goal was to insure that no heirs would survive Papa or Samuel. That's when Papa and the Hopegivers International Board decided that the boys and I should be moved to the United States for safety reasons.

I knew early on in my marriage to Samuel how committed he is to God's calling. For both of us, it is a calling and not a career. Within two weeks of our arrival in India (July 1986) as newlyweds, he was traveling several days a month. I had to learn early on to spend large chunks of time alone, but those times gave me the opportunity to grow spiritually by studying the Bible and reading many amazing biographies of God's chosen servants who served Him on the mission field. I spent time learning the language, learning to cook Indian food, and being a hostess to volunteers that would come and stay anywhere from 2 days to 6 months. I also learned to depend on the Lord for everyday needs, guidance, and fellowship. But it was still lonely.

After returning to the United States – September 2001 until February 2006 - we experienced an unexpected blessing as a family. During that period of time, Samuel could spend 4-6 weeks at a time here in the states with us. We actually had more time together as a family than ever before. When we lived in India, there were people around 24/7. Here in the states, we have a more normal family life.

I love it when Samuel is here with us, because we do what families do. We cook and eat together; even clean up together. The boys are calmer when he is around - typical of boys and their fathers. He is stricter with them and expects things to be done the first time he asks. When I ask, it gets done, eventually. I don't get on their case a lot, although I probably should. I might be doing them a disservice because I'm not a disciplinarian like Samuel. I think – like many mothers – I tend to overcompensate for the boys not having their father around on a regular basis. They have gotten used to Dad being on trips for the ministry. It's all they have ever known.

By the grace of God and through the prayers of many, the boys are growing and developing into well-rounded young men. Our prayers for them are that they will each hear and heed the call of God for their own lives and then follow that path.

The boys stay very busy and they keep me running between school, church, soccer, baseball, basketball, choir and guitar lessons. I am grateful to our Pastor, Don Wilhite of Calvary Baptist Church and to Calvary Christian School for their support and encouragement to our family. I am comforted in knowing that the boys are surrounded by loving

Christian leaders at the school. Our boys are blessed to have an education in such a wonderful school.

# CHAPTER 4:

## Samuel: Solitary Confinement

They continued to interrogate me 24 hours a day for the first 14 days after my arrest. I was not allowed any sleep during that period. Whenever an official was in the room questioning me, I was made to sit on the bare cement floor. Whenever I was left alone, I was forced to stand up and lean against a wall in order to keep me from falling asleep. Although I am grateful they didn't beat me, the lack of sleep was almost as unbearable. If I began to doze off, they would either burn me with their cigarettes or throw hot coffee on me. I was given bread once a day and some water as needed.

I was never allowed to have an attorney during this time period, even though it is a law in India that a lawyer must be present when a prisoner is being questioned. Evidently the law meant nothing to them when it came to my rights. Every two or three days they would take me out of detention and escort me the 15 kilometers to the court house. I was always escorted by a group of police commandos bearing arms due to the constant threat of a sniper attack.

I was forced to sit on the bare floor 17 hours a day during that 14 day period. The average daily temperature at that time was around 115 degrees. They would ask me the same questions over and over again. My body and mind were broken. The faces of my father, my wife and my sons continuously swam before my eyes. The frightened faces of the destitute and orphaned children haunted me. During these first 14 days, I was also concerned about the condition of Mr. R. S. Nair – Emmanuel's Administrator; Mr. V. S. Thomas – Director of the Kota orphanage; Nathaniel Dennis – who translated the book **Haqeeqat** from English to Hindi; and the young student, Vikram Kindo who managed the book stand in the library at the Bible College. We had not yet laid eyes on one another, but I knew they were in the jail somewhere. They were one of the reasons I was in Noida when I was arrested. My plan was to post bail for them. I knew they had to be undergoing a lot of mental pressure in jail – all because they were employees of the ministry.

I also knew that an arrest warrant had been issued for my father. They had declared him a dangerous criminal. There were large posters of his photograph taped on buses and trains asking for his whereabouts. My heart trembled when I thought of my elderly father being treated with the abuse I was experiencing. I knew the police were searching for him every day. What would it take to appease the religious militants? How many children and servants of God would need to suffer before this hatred toward Christianity would come to a halt?

The first time I was escorted to court under police protection, a large crowd of anti-Christians organized a rally against me. They shouted slogans which were designed to poison the hearts and minds of the general public against the ministry. Their numbers overwhelmed the court whenever they became aware of my presence there. I became choice entertainment for the anti-Christian crowds who would show up whenever I was transported between the jail and the court house. The media enjoyed great ratings at my expense during those days. You can probably guess my state of mind at this time. They had only one aim – my end. Yet I knew that:

*"For me to live is Christ, and to die is gain."*
*Philippians 1:21*

Rajasthan actually declared a day off from work for the entire state so people could attend these hate rallies. The city of Kota was literally closed down. In one day, the anti-Christians burned 93 effigies of me and my father. It spurred a micro-industry for people creating the effigies! They were hung on buildings and on bridges. People took turns beating the effigies with sticks before burning them. This continued for days.

*"And you shall be hated of all men for My name's sake. But there shall not a*
*hair of your head perish. In your patience possess your souls."*
*Luke 21:17-19*

To this day, I am grateful to the National Human Rights Commission and the government officials for supplying the security that kept me safe during this tense period. I kept a smile on my face whenever I was in the public eye. The newspaper reporters would comment, "What is the secret behind the smile on Dr. Samuel's face?" Of course, only a child of the King would know that secret. The words of Jesus brought me comfort during this stressful period.

*"Blessed are you, when men shall hate you, and when they shall separate you from their company, and shall reproach you, and cast out your name as evil, for the Son of man's (Jesus) sake. Rejoice you in that day, and leap for joy, for behold, your reward is great in heaven..." Luke 6:22-23*

On the trips back and forth between the jail and the court house, my friends would walk alongside me. The local police – who did the escorting – didn't seem threatened by the interaction between me and my friends.

During the first few days of my detention in Kota, an Indian journalist acquired permission to interview me. While we were talking, we kept hearing a beeping sound. The journalist was adamant that the police locate what and where the sound was coming from. They eventually found an explosive device hidden in another room near where the journalist and I had been sitting. I thanked God that the journalist convinced the police to locate the source of the sound. The police were able to diffuse the explosive.

On March 29, my application for bail was rejected by the Lower Court. That's when the guards decided to assign me to my own cell. A request came into the facility strongly suggesting that I not be put with the general population in the prison. Evidently, the radicals had arranged to have some of their men arrested so they would be in prison while I was there. Their orders were to kill me.

I remember the police escorting me through room number one and shutting the door behind us, then room number two, and shutting the door behind us. They took a left turn, and room number three became my cell – a 3' x 5' concrete dungeon. At this point I had not slept in 14 days and nights and now they were putting me in a cell with no light, no air – not even a ceiling fan. It is 120 degrees and I have a room that is not even big enough for me to lie down. They said, "This is your room." They tossed me into the cell and shut the door behind them. All I could say was, "Lord, I have no idea why you are doing this to me and I have no idea what you want me to do." I sat in that room and started crying. It was the first time I had cried in 14 days.

Now that I was in a cell, they were no longer keeping me from sleep, but sleep was still impossible. As soon as it was dark outside, the mosquitoes and rats would attack me with a vengeance. I guess a rat had set up housekeeping in one corner of the cell; he clearly considered me to be the intruder. Not knowing what kind of animal it was because it was so dark in there, I could only feel it moving around the room. I tried to grab it. I knew that whatever it was, it was certainly big. When I did finally catch it, I killed it. It was perhaps 20 -25 hours later when this thing I killed began to stink.

Finally, a guard came to check on me. He asked, "Mr. Thomas, are you okay?" I said, "Not really. Would you bring your flashlight in here?" He didn't have a flashlight with him, but he did have matches because he had been smoking marijuana. He lit a match and came into my room. He said, "Uh-oh, you killed our god." I had killed a very big rat. My only response to him was, "What kind of a god is this if you can kill it with your bare hands?" I shouldn't have said that. He went straight to the media and told them that I had insulted the Hindu gods. As a result of my careless response, more orphans were beaten; pastors were kicked out of their churches and the churches burned down. It became clear that I had to guard my tongue. To this day I have scars on my legs from that cranky roommate I killed.

Because rats are considered one of the Hindu gods, people catch them, but they do not kill them. They catch them in cages with spring loaded doors and release them outside. As punishment for killing one of their gods, the police brought the cages from the kitchen and released the rats into my cell. They released 14 in all. The door to my cell was wooden

so they would back the cages up against the door
and when they unlatched the spring-loaded
doors on the cages, the rats would run under the
wooden door and into my cell. I know this
because I could hear the trap doors snap shut after
each rat scurried into my cell.

At my lowest points I found myself asking - no one
in particular - what crime I had committed to
deserve such a hell hole. My only crime was
dedicating my life to helping lepers, orphans, and
the poor – regardless of their religious beliefs –
become responsible and productive citizens for
India. Who would have ever thought that caring for
orphans and widows would be such a threat to
anyone? If I had known 25 years ago that my
reward for serving the oppressed of India would be
humiliation, insult and rejection, I seriously doubt
that I would have taken this path. I guess that is why
Christ only "gives a lamp unto our feet". He gives
us just enough information so we have the courage
to persevere for the next few moments or days. I
know this to be true because 25 years after making
my commitment to the mission field, I am willing to
go to prison as punishment for serving the
oppressed. If necessary, I am willing to lay down
my life. I praise God for what He does in the heart
of self-centered man!

The hatred towards the ministry had been escalating
for some time. When we were only
graduating 100-200 Bible students a year and
sending them out into the mission field, I guess we

weren't seen as a threat. But in more recent times, literally thousands are graduating each year from the Bible College and the Bible Institutes – all of them with a passion for spreading the Gospel of Jesus Christ throughout India.

When I joined Dad in 1986, we had 210 churches. Now over 43,000 churches have been planted. Great success for God's Kingdom is the very stuff that stirs the enemy up and makes him angry. We shouldn't be shocked at these recent events.

Jesus is in me and in my outside circumstances. He knows just how much Samuel can bear. Have you ever seen a one-armed potter? No, they use both arms. One hand and arm is inside the clay vessel while the other is outside the vessel forming its shape. The hand outside is careful not to use more force on the outside than he knows the hand inside the vessel can bear before the clay pot breaks. God is the same. Jesus' hand is inside me and He is also in my outside circumstances. He knows just how much Samuel can bear. I will tell you that my Jesus has never abandoned me!

Worry about my colleagues who were also in jail was eating at me. I wanted to know how they were faring. I prayed I could be locked up with them so we could have spiritual fellowship. No one would tell me where they had been taken.

What I did know was that sleep deprivation was a major part of my torture. It was impossible to shut my eyes, even momentarily, for fear of the mosquitoes or the rat droppings falling into my drinking water or the rats eating what little food I was given. The smell of the rats and their filthy bodies was disgusting. During the day, when temperatures were extremely hot, I had to wrap the blanket around my body to escape the bites of the rats. They were relentless. It didn't matter whether I was sitting or standing. They would run up and down my body. The blanket was filthy from their urine.

Due to soaring temperatures I was constantly bathed in sweat. My tiny cell did not have a toilet, so I did whatever I could to answer nature's call. When one of the bolder rats bit my toe, I vowed to wear my shoes day and night even though the shoes only added to the heat of my body. I had no choice if I was going to protect my feet.

I was living a nightmare. I was truly in a kind of hell. Frequently, tears would fall uncontrollably down my cheeks. The Holy Spirit was always faithful to remind me of Bible heroes like Job, Paul, and Peter - and especially our Lord and Savior, Jesus. He bore humiliation, insult and great torture and agony to become a sacrifice for us. I would then recall the many great men throughout history who also bore much anguish and distress when they were jailed, and some even martyred. Great men like Mahatma Gandhi, Vinod Bhave, and Jawaharlal Nehru – all of them great leaders and each a founding father of my great nation. All were jailed for the cause of truth. It is said that "Truth can be subjected to persecution, but not subjugated." This understanding gave me strength and courage as well. Truth will be tested, but never defeated!

God did not put me in prison, but He allowed me and my colleagues to be imprisoned. We always have choices. I wanted to find the strength to turn my prison cell into a room of praise. I would recall the story of Joseph in the Old Testament. God moved him from the pit to prison and from a prison to a palace. Even so, the loneliness, the physical harassment, and the emotional torment shook me to the core. No one knew the horrendous condition I was living under. There was no one to talk to during the hours upon hours I was relegated to spend in that tiny, sweltering cell. I finally lost it and began weeping uncontrollably in this dungeon they called a cell.

Once I was assigned to this cell, they kept me locked up for 38 straight hours. Finally, they gave me an opportunity to go to the toilet. I was taken to another cell which had an attached bathroom where – I praised God – I saw where the other three servants of God were being kept. When I saw these men of God, I felt as though I were in the presence of angels – not mere men. Led by the Spirit in those first few seconds, I said to them, "We are privileged that we have been counted worthy to suffer humiliation for the Lord." That was the only exchange we had, because the sentry would not allow us to communicate further with one another.

As I was led out of their cell, I noticed that they had a fan overhead. From the depths of my heart I prayed that God would place me in the same cell as these men of God. I would have a toilet, a fan to relieve the horrendous heat, and my loneliness would be gone. The sentry stood guard as I used the toilet. They still would not give me permission to shower, but I praised the Lord for what was allowed.

Within 10 minutes I was taken back to my hellish cell and locked up once again. Alone and without my Bible, I could not even read Scripture in order to draw in some spiritual strength. I prayed to the Lord, "Please, send me one Bible." Friends, my Lord heard that prayer! The very next morning when I was taken to the toilet, Brother Nathaniel Dennis said to me, *1Thessalonians 5:16-18*. Although the two sentries heard the words, they did not understand the meaning, but I did! Because I knew the verse, I realized that God was using the mouth of His servant to encourage me to stay firm in the purpose of the Lord's will. As soon as Brother Nathaniel's words fell on my ears, God's Word echoed in my heart:

> *"Rejoice evermore. Pray without ceasing. In*
> *everything give thanks: for this*
> *is the will of God in Christ Jesus concerning you."*
> *1 Thessalonians 5:16-18*

I thanked God over and over again for these words. This then reminded me of the words from *James 1:2-5:*

*"Consider it pure joy, my brothers, whenever you face trials of many kinds, because you know that the testing of your faith develops perseverance. Perseverance must finish its work so that you may be mature and complete, not lacking anything."*

*"Blessed is the man who perseveres under trial, because when he has stood the test, he will receive the crown of life that God has promised to those who love him." James 1: 12*

Friends, I tell you from the bottom of my heart that these words anchored themselves into my heart.

I was given permission to bathe the next day and as I came out of the shower area, Brother Nathaniel handed me a Gideon's New Testament from behind the bars of his cell. The guard did not object to my taking it. I was so grateful to God for His provision. I was led back to my cell and enclosed in my own personal hell once again. But this time it was different. I hungrily opened my Bible and was stunned to discover that this was the same Bible that we had distributed to prisoners just five years ago. They had accepted the Bibles and put them in the jail library. I learned later that my colleagues had demanded that the officials give Brother Nathaniel a

Bible from the library. When I saw where this Bible came from, I realized that what I had intended as good for the prisoners five years earlier, had now become a blessing for me.

*"The Lord has magnified His Word above all His name." Psalm 138:2*

I read the Bible as long as the first door was left open and I had light. I spent many hours each day standing upright reading in this grim cell. Whenever I attempted to lie down, an army of rats would swarm over me. Their odor gave me a splitting headache. My legs were swollen because I was standing on them for so many hours. I was in a lot of pain. I had mosquito bites all over my body – my back was covered in hives. Sleep was simply out of the question, in spite of the fact that I had already been awake for 84 hours plus the 14 days when I was in police custody. I was desperate for some sleep, but the cruelty of my surroundings kept my sleep interrupted. There were dark circles under my red and swollen eyes. The intense heat in my cell had drained my body of necessary moisture; I knew that I was becoming dangerously dehydrated.

The faces of my old father, my wife Shelley, and my two sons – Steven and Timothy – were constantly before my eyes. I didn't know how they were handling all that was going on. I was certain that they did not know the misery I was living in daily. In my loneliest moments, with tears running down my cheeks, I would hum a song I composed

26 years earlier in Hindi. This song helped to reassure and calm me during these lonely times. The words of this song would pour from my lips. This is the English translation:

*My Jesus, how great is Your love, greater than the stars in the sky; the mountain and seas. In difficulties, when life is discouraging I call on the Lord, "Pour out Your mercy upon me. "Before I offer my prayers, He says, "I am with you."*

Although written in 1980, somehow this song filled my heart with hope. It became a testimony of my grief as I sat in solitary confinement. I knew that it pleased God, and that we are always in His will when we bear suffering for good (*1Peter 1:20*).

# CHAPTER 5

## Samuel: Waiting on God Together

On the 17th day of my confinement, I was removed from my abysmal cell and put in with my colleagues. I was so happy. For the first time since my arrest I was given real food to eat instead of a single serving of bread to last a whole day. That night I lay my broken, tired, weak body on the floor and slept my first deep sleep.

I couldn't stop thanking God for His mercies. At last all four of us – Mr. Nair had already been released because he was not a Christian – were locked up in the same room. The four of us would spend our time singing praises to God throughout the day, reading the Bible, meditating and encouraging one another with what we had read in Scripture.

All of our families were worried for our safety and were praying continuously for our release. Churches from every corner of the globe were fasting and praying. All of us understood the source of this persecution. This was a battle between the ruler of darkness and the people of God. In spite of what it looked like on the outside, this was a spiritual battle. The three brothers who were with me in prison prayed daily with me: "O Lord, may Your name only be glorified through this captivity of ours. May You increase while we decrease."

I remember an incident that happened to my father in 1967. He told me that he had been beaten by a group of anti-Christians and put into the Kota jail for sharing the Gospel. The irony of my situation was not lost. Here I sit, his son, 39 years later in the same jail, and for the very same reason. At that moment, I couldn't help but reflect on how much things had not really changed.

By the first of April, both lower courts of the District Court had rejected our bail applications. Our case was actually more media-driven than anything else. The media made it look as though we were against the Hindu people, even though it was not true. Since the bail applications were rejected we had to remain in custody.

Shortly after the lower courts had rejected our bail applications, Brother V. S. Thomas submitted his application for bail to the High Court. It was also rejected. He then applied to the Supreme Court and they granted him interim bail. He was released, but put under house arrest.

Unfortunately, funds would have been wasted on this legal move for me. Unless the High Court would deny bail for me, I could not take my case to the Supreme Court where I had a chance for release. The High Court continued to delay their decision where I was concerned, so they could prevent me from moving my request up to the Supreme Court. Since the Supreme Court approved the bail application for my father and Mr. V. S. Thomas, the local police were fairly certain that they would grant me bail as well. That was simply not going to happen if they could help it. If it were not for the generous people of God in India and abroad, we would not have had the funds to help us continue to fight this legal battle. I praise God daily for all who continue to help us pay the legal costs, as the battle goes on, even now.

Although the police protected me from the mobs outside, the inmates in the jail also disliked me! As I walked by their cells, they would curse at me and threaten me. I always kept a calm demeanor. It didn't matter whether I was in the court room or in jail.

Around the 19th or 20th day of incarceration, a guard came into our cell and said, "Here's a newspaper for you, Mr. Thomas." You can ask Shelley. I don't read the newspaper, but now it is being delivered to me in prison! The newspaper was full of, "Samuel Thomas arrested; Samuel Thomas said this about the Hindu gods; Samuel Thomas, Samuel Thomas. I mean, the whole newspaper was filled with bad press about the ministry. I asked the guard, "Who sent this newspaper?" The guard said, "There's a guy named Patrick who is from England. He was arrested three years ago for doing drugs. He sent this newspaper to you because he also reads the English newspaper. He knows that you will read this newspaper; there's nobody else who speaks

English in this prison." I said, "Okay, tell him thanks."

As I came out of my shower that day, I noticed something strange about an advertisement in the newspaper. It had handwriting all over it. When I took a closer look, I realized that Patrick had written me a note. It said, "I've always questioned the virgin birth of Christ. I've always questioned how Jesus can forgive our sins? I have been praying for you ever since I learned that they were going to arrest you. I'm glad to know that you're safe and alive in this prison. Would you answer these questions for me?" I looked at the other three pastors and said, "How does one answer these questions?" I asked the guard if I could borrow his pen. He said, "One dollar." I told him that I didn't have any money, but that I would pay him when I was released. He gave me the pen and I started writing. Every morning at 10am the newspaper would come. By 3:30pm the newspaper would go back to Patrick. Everyday we would dialogue using the newspaper. He would say things like, "In the book of Isaiah, I don't understand this…" Then he would start quoting Scriptures.

By the 47th day, Patrick had written me a beautiful note. He said, "Mr. Samuel Thomas, I'm so glad that God brought you to the prison. I've accepted Jesus Christ as my personal Savior and Lord." I felt like a charismatic! I'm telling you, I had an incredible worship time in my cell that day. I told the Lord, "Please forgive me for ever questioning

You; forgive me for ever doubting You. How can I not praise You with my life?" In the prison - without a microphone and without a church building - God is saving people! Oh, I was so excited. The three pastors said, "I don't think you want to leave, Samuel." I said, "Not if God is going to do this kind of work!"

Sleep continued to escape all of us. We counted ourselves fortunate if we got one hour of uninterrupted sleep. Even with the overhead fan, my colleagues and I experienced extreme heat in our cell. An electric bulb hung overhead and burned 24 hours a day which only added to the sweltering heat. The yellowish luminescent glow from the incandescent lamp was harmful to our eyes. They kept light on us 24/7 along with a closed circuit camera in our cell so they could monitor our movements. We were given old dusty, frayed blankets, which were full of holes. We would wet our blankets and towels so we could wrap ourselves in them to get some relief from the heat. The plates and the tumblers we ate and drank from were earthen. They did put an earthen pot inside our cell so we could store some drinking water.

To add to the unbearable environment, the guards would come around to the cell every two hours and rattle the heavy iron padlocks shouting, "How many of you are there? How are you?" If we had managed to drop off to sleep, this would wake all of us up. The fatigue we all experienced was becoming critical. Oh, to have just one night of uninterrupted sleep! To add to the torment, there were still the rats, mosquitoes, crickets, cockroaches, and ants to deal with, and they were relentless. We killed as many as we could with our shoes, but there just seemed to be an unending supply of the critters.

One day they brought another prisoner into our cell so he could repair the light. He asked us some very strange questions. "Don't you feel scared to be in this cell? Don't you have nightmares and bad dreams? Isn't the ghostly presence giving you the creeps?" We told him that we were all fine and that we weren't having any of the problems he mentioned. I must admit, he aroused our curiosity. We asked him why he was asking. He said, "Many of the previous prisoners who had occupied this particular cell in the past had committed suicide."

We told him that, "We are servants of the living Lord – Jesus Christ – and we fear only Him. We had not been attacked by any demons and fully expected that we would not be bothered by them in the future. Besides, our Lord has given us authority over the powers of Satan so we will not be harmed by any spiritual demons. Our God knows even the number of hairs on our heads." We had to remember that "greater is He who is within you than he who is in the world."

After he left our cell, we talked about what we had been told. This was simply another ploy by the enemy to discourage us. It is important that we always remember that the enemy wages his war primarily against our minds. He wants us to be afraid, to lose faith, and to live preoccupied with worry. He wants us to place our trust in mortal man and forsake the Lord Jesus Christ. The Lord encourages us with the following words in Scripture:

*"For God has not given us the spirit of fear; but of power, and of love, and of a sound mind." 2 Timothy 1:7*

The food and tea served to inmates is minimal and of poor quality. God blessed our shortage of food through food packets that believers managed to bring us. We thanked God for these blessings.

Since both of the lower courts had rejected our bail applications, and the High Court continued to delay their decision, we had no idea if we would ever be released from jail. But our God is so faithful to encourage – even in what appears to be impossible circumstances. On April 2, 2006 we read a Scripture that spoke directly to each of our hearts.

*"Then they made Jason and the others post bond and let them go." Acts 17:9*

We thanked God for this verse and believed that it was His assurance that we would eventually be released. We claimed this verse for ourselves and prayed it as a promise from Him to us every day.

We began to thank Him for our release, even though it had not yet taken place!

We learned that the reason the lower courts rejected our bail applications was that the section of the Indian penal code under which our cases had been filed, did not have a provision for bail. This meant that we had no chance for bail unless the court decided to release us on bail at its own discretion. Unfortunately, the pressure from certain factions concerning our case was so strong that we could not get justice. The anti-Christians filed legal cases against us under this particular penal code because they knew that bail would not be allowed. Their goal was to keep us locked up for three years which would give them plenty of time to confiscate all of the ministry properties. This would then force the orphans back onto the streets to resume a life of despair and darkness from which they had been rescued. They had already made arrangements to auction off all the lands belonging to the ministry in the short time we had been imprisoned. From where we sat, things looked pretty grim. We continually reminded one another that the Lord released Paul, Silas and Jason (*Acts 17:9*) and He could do the same for us.

Near the end of April, Vikram – who was only 16 at the time – was moved to a juvenile facility while the court waited for a relative to come and sign paperwork on his behalf.

My application for bail was set for another hearing. It was to take place on Monday, May 1, at 10:30am. On that day we fasted and prayed while Brother Nathaniel read from the Bible. Suddenly, a breeze from the ceiling fan caused the pages of the Bible to turn. The page fell open to *Psalm 54*. Although the ceiling fan continued to turn, the pages never turned again. We began to read this Psalm. *Psalm 54* is a prayer of David which asks God to save him from his enemies. We prayed David's prayer as our own prayer. As the clock in the jail struck 7 am, we read this Psalm once again. It was our prayer of rescue. I remember how the seventh verse filled us with joy the last time we read it that day. The verse read:

*"For He has delivered me out of all trouble: and
mine eye hath seen its
desire upon mine enemies."*

Finally, they came to get me and take me to the Lower Court in Kota where I was presented before the judge. As I was being led into the courtroom, the word of deliverance that had come to us from God that very morning began to resonate in my heart. It was so persistent that I had to believe it. Dear friends, what I believed did come true!

As I stood in the presence of the judge that day, my advocate received a call on his cell phone. I had been granted interim bail by the High Court. The Lower Court judge was ordered to release me from custody. The lawyer gave me the good news immediately. I cannot begin to express in words how excited I was at that moment. I could not stop thanking God. When I was returned to my cell, I shared the good news with Brother Nathaniel. We both cried tears of joy, giving thanks to God for fulfilling the word He had given us that very morning.

As I waited for my release, I recalled a few Christian brothers who did not believe I would ever leave jail. There were many, so called Christians, who wanted us to stay in jail. They had even submitted photos of Dad and me baptizing a few of the adult orphans in hopes of antagonizing the anti-Christian element. By God's grace, it did not work against us. Hearing about such things was very discouraging in those days.

Friends, this is why Jesus says, "Take heed what you hear." *Mark 4:23-24*. Faith can so easily be damaged by listening to man, even men who don't mean any harm to you. Who do you listen to – man or God? Whenever you are in any kind of trouble, pick your advisors very carefully. We must always choose to trust in the Word of the Lord and accept God at His word. *Psalm 138:2* says:

> *"...for You have magnified Your Word above Your entire name."*

On the very day I was released from jail, an old man came to our cell. He said, "Sam, we missed celebrating Easter Sunday. Can we have a worship meeting today?" I said, "Sure, but I can't let you in. Our cell is locked from the outside." He said, "Well, I know people in here and they will open the door." Someone did come and open the door so he could join us. He introduced himself – I can't mention his name. He told me that he was 75 years old and had been the secretary of a church in India. He looked at me and said, "Let's worship the Lord together." And we did that day! We just praised the Lord with everything in us and then we began to share with this man everything that God had been doing in our lives. The next thing I know, this old man is on his knees, grabbing my hands and saying, "I have never accepted Jesus Christ as my Savior and Lord. I want to do that right now." It was wonderful having the privilege of leading one more soul to Christ while I was in jail!

The moment this man finished the sinner's prayer, two guards came to our cell. One of them announced, "Mr. Thomas, you are free today." With all that God was doing in the jail, I felt like I didn't want to leave. Of course, I didn't say those words. Yet I was torn as I saw the great things God was doing in that prison!

Nathaniel had to stay in the jail for another month. He was put in with the general population and was abused and mistreated by the other prisoners. He did not retaliate; he simply prayed for them. After a while he gained their respect and they told him that they knew he couldn't have disrespected or insulted their gods. Within days of my release, the ceiling fan in our cell crashed to the floor in the exact spot that I would sit day after day while in the prison. What marvelous protection from the Lord!

The grace of God was present before He ever called me into the ministry. When I was in prison, and in the toughest circumstances, He was there. He never left me. He fulfilled His promise,

*"I will never leave you or forsake you."*

# Chapter 6

## Samuel's Freedom: God's Way and His Timing

On May 2, 2006 at 12:00 noon, I was released from jail after 49 days of intense suffering. But our God never wastes anything – regardless of how it looks in the natural. During our 49 days of incarceration, the Lord opened a way for us to put New Testament Bibles in the hands of the other prison inmates.

A high ranking leader of an anti-Christian group was jailed as a suspect in a murder case right around the time I was arrested. He had an intense hatred for us, but we were given an opportunity to meet with him while we were in prison. He allowed us to share our faith with him. By the end of our first meeting, he admitted that his leaders evidently did not know the truth about Christianity. What they told him about us would cause anyone to loathe us.

Unfortunately, most members of the anti-Christian groups in India have been brainwashed. This man was in prison because he joined one such anti-Christian group and committed heinous crimes in the name of stomping out Christianity. His life was now ruined, and his family devastated.

He told us that he had noticed the difference between his heart and ours. He said, "You are in prison just like me, but your face is radiant and peaceful! I know the truth about why you have been arrested and put in prison. It is because of political hatred. I also know that religion is the instrument being used to incite the crowds so they will attack you."

I gave this man a Gospel tract to read. Now, you might be wondering how I acquired Gospel tracts in jail. Believers brought copies of the New Testament and some Bible tracts in to be put into the prison library. Permission was given. We would take the material from the library and distribute it to interested inmates. Our Lord is a Lord who causes good things to happen in bad situations.

*"And we know that all things work together for good to them that love God, to them who are called according to His purpose."*
*Romans 8:28*

It is always according to His will that the Gospel be actively shared - whether in normal circumstances or in persecution. The Gospel message is powerful and when that power manifests itself, the people recognize the way of salvation and choose to follow that path.

A known gangster and murderer – upon entering the jail - let me know that he would kill me the first chance he got. He asked me what the word conversion meant. He said, "I hear all these anti-Christians saying that you are converting orphaned children to Christianity. What does this conversion mean?"

Honestly, *I* dislike the word "conversion". I never use the word, so I had to make up a definition very quickly. I said, "Conversion is when God takes the dirty heart and replaces it with a new heart. He gives Himself to us." I found myself telling him what the ministry does. "We take the children born to the prostitutes, the children that live on the streets with no parents and the children of lepers, and bring them into the fear and knowledge of the Lord Jesus Christ. Then we send them out as leaders." The next thing I know, this man who wanted to kill me, has tears running down his face. He looks up at me and says, "Well, that's a good story, Mr. Thomas, but don't think I'm going to change my mind about killing you."

As we sat in the courthouse waiting for our cases to be heard, this same murderer says, "A lot of people have come to see you today." There were a lot of Hopegivers pastors and many orphans present. Then he asked, "What is that book you distribute on the street?" I said, "It is the New Testament." He asked, "Can you ask one of your pastors to get some for me and my friends?" I said, "Sure, how many do you need?" He said, "28." I said, "Okay." I didn't know if this was just a scam, but under the circumstances I thought, so what! So I asked one of the pastors to bring 28 New Testaments to the jail. Since a visitor cannot give anything to prisoners, the guards had to bring them into this man and his friends.

The next time I was being escorted to the courthouse, I could see this man behind the bars. He yelled to me, "Thomas, that's a boring book. You got something with pictures?" And I said, "Yeah, we have something with pictures. We have a book called **He Lived Among Us**." He said, "Bring it." I asked him how many he needed. He said, "I just found out there are 1,500 inmates. Bring us 1,500." I said, "Really?" He said, "Yeah." I said, "I can't bring them in myself." He said, "Just tell the guards and they will bring them to me." Because the guards are afraid of this man and his cronies, they brought the 1,500 copies of **He Lived Among Us** into the prison. The very next day the media had a field day with that information. Now they wanted to "Get Samuel Thomas out of jail before he converts all the inmates to Christianity." Oh, what a joy. Only God - only God could do this.

Shelley came over to India about a week after I was released from prison. Although we were finally granted interim bail, our troubles were far from over. Within three weeks of being released, the enemies filed a fresh case against Dad and me and were arranging to have arrest warrants issued. Now we were being charged as traitors.

After picking Shelley up at the airport, we went to Kota. We were there for 14 hours during which time the High Court at Jaipur granted me permission to visit the United States for a month. Simultaneously, this new case was filed against us and plans were in motion to arrest and jail us once again. We received news of our pending arrest and left Kota immediately by car. The police were unyielding. They were single-minded in their goal to re-arrest us. They remained only steps behind us as we fled. Their goal was to keep us from leaving the state of Rajasthan, but the Lord had other plans! Even though there were police bearing AK 47 rifles randomly stopping cars in order to find us, the Lord seemingly placed a veil over their eyes as we drove right past them.

We received news the next day that the police assumed we would head for the airport in Jaipur. They secured the airport in order to capture us when we arrived. They notified all the other airports across India that we were to be stopped at all costs. More than 40 police personnel arrived at the airport where we were scheduled to fly out that next day.

At midnight, it became clear that we had no choice, but to go into hiding. Once again, we began the process of applying for bail so we could prevent arrest. And once again, the Lower Courts refused our bail application. By this time we had gone underground. My wife Shelley had to fly back to the United States alone – once again. I would not see her for another 12 long months.

The police kept watch at the airports for over 10 days. They then shifted their search for us to Delhi. By then we had fled from there as well. The only joy I did have during this period was that my aged, godly father and a few Christian brothers were with me during this time. We spent our days in hiding, reading the Bible, meditating, singing and praying. We learned of the extensive campaign launched against us in Rajasthan through the newspapers and television.

# Chapter 7

## Shelley: Returning Home without Samuel

Once I knew Samuel had been granted temporary bail, I flew to India. My gut told me that they would not really allow him to come to the United States after his release. I wanted to see him before the next wave of persecution began – whatever that might be. If I hadn't gone then, I wouldn't have seen him for 14 months and I wasn't willing to risk that either.

The new warrant that was being proposed for Samuel and my father-in-law now accused them of being anti-nationalists. These people were determined to get Samuel back into jail again. The information that we heard claimed that the police only wanted to question Samuel, but if that were actually true, they could still hold him for hours or even days. We weren't willing to take that risk, so going into hiding was his only option. We had already planned to leave Kota the next day in order to catch a flight for the United States. When we learned of the pending warrant, we left at four in the morning so Samuel could not be brought in for questioning.

During our trip to escape Samuel's arrest, soldiers carrying AK 47's would randomly stop cars looking for us. It almost felt like we were invisible, because our car was never chosen.

I remember stopping at one point on the drive to Delhi to get some tea. We thought it would give Samuel a needed break since he was so tired. While we waited to be served our tea, he fell asleep sitting at the table in the restaurant. We picked up the latest newspaper that day so we could read what the governor had decided to do about the newly proposed Freedom of Religion Act. By God's grace, the governor had refused to sign it. This Act would require that if someone wanted to convert to another religion, they had to get permission from the leader of their previous religious affiliation. God's plans are never thwarted. It was not long after the governor refused to sign this act that she became the President!

I only saw Samuel for four days in May. He was supposed to come back with me, but because of this new warrant, I had to leave him in hiding and fly home alone. I did not lay eyes on him again until April 2007. While Samuel was in hiding all those months, he would call me from time to time and let me know he was safe.

I know that there were many people at the time who thought Samuel should return to the United States so he wouldn't be arrested again. But I know my husband. If he had come home just to save his own skin, he would be haunted by the faces of orphans who would be back on the streets starving and being abused – and so would I. He could never live with himself knowing that his actions caused harm to the orphans. His heart had no choice but to go back to

Dr. Samuel and his father Dr. M.A. Thomas preaching at the 2005 graduation.

Shelley Thomas before the persecution.

Samuel - March - May 2006. Coming back from a court hearing during his time in police custody.

Samuel - March - May 2006. Going from courthouse back to jail.

Samuel - March - May 2006. Leaving courthouse.

Samuel -March - May 2006. In jeep, light blue shirt.

Samuel - March - May 2006 Leaving courthouse after hearing that his appeal for bail was rejected.

Funeral of G. Israel, one of the pastors stabbed to death during the persecution.

Samuel - March to May 2006.

Samuel - March - May 2006, Just before being handed over to judicial custody.

Samuel - March - May 2006. Entering the central jail.

Samuel - March - May 2006. Police taking Samuel to another court hearing.

Samuel -March - May 2006 outside of vehicle in which they were escorting him.

Samuel -March - May 2006 Brought to court in vehicle due to riots. Not bullet proof but safer than other vehicles against the rocks being thrown.

Samuel, May 2,2006, released from jail.

Samuel- May 2, 2006. His release from jail and talking to pastors soon after release.

Samuel - May 2, 2006, released from jail.

Samuel and his grandfather May 2, 2006, shortly after his release from jail.

Visiting Delhi Orphanage after being released from prison.

Sharing the Gospel with two of the lepers in the leper colony.

Thomas Family - July 2010

India when this all began. God just does not allow him to cut and run!

# CHAPTER 8

## Samuel: The Financial Toll during the Persecution

I do not hold any grievances against the officials who arrested me in March of 2006. It was clear to me then and continues to be clear today that this is the work of Satan and his army. A common enemy to us all, he is eaten up with hatred and is determined to destroy Hopegivers International and all other organizations like it. I still can't believe the tool – the innocent sale of a book – they used to launch their outrageous persecution. I guess the enemy doesn't care how lame the accusation, as long as it is effective.

How did the government even discover we had the book in our library? At the October, 2005 General Convention we had set up a bookstand – something we do at every convention – and opened it to the public so they could purchase books. A constable from the police station dressed in civilian clothes visited our book stand and found the book **Haqeeqat** among all the books we had for sale. He paid the young Bible student tending the book stand 200 rupees and acquired a receipt for his purchase, as proof of where he had bought the book.

Government officials, who have the book in their possession, are fully aware that the charges against me and my father are false. In fact, we learned that a reporter, who was snooping around, discovered excerpts taken from Mr. Matthew's book. These excerpts had been altered so that they would sound like insults. Someone then published these altered excerpts as a pamphlet and labeled our ministry as the publisher. Government officials do know who manipulated and printed this information.

In January, the anti-Christian factions started to create a new set of rumors against us. We could see that holding the February convention would further tear at the very fabric of brotherhood we had established within the community. We cancelled the Kota February, 2006 convention in hopes of maintaining some peace and stability in the area. We chose to cooperate with the government's request to cancel in spite of the great loss – both financially and spiritually - to the ministry. In spite of our efforts, it did not quell the hatred which ultimately culminated into the most heinous and long-term persecution that we have ever faced.

The fundamentalists went so far as to organize a large state picket (called a bund) which demanded that the officials arrest Dad and me. The whole community of Kota was a tinder box ready to explode due to all the tension. It seemed like every street corner had someone burning effigies of Dad and me. They even had rallies organized so they could attract others who would listen to their accusations and join forces with them. We were told that in just one day, there were 93 effigies of our images burned!

While I was still imprisoned, the conspiracy to destroy the ministry began to roll out its plan very quickly.

*First*, they cancelled the registrations (*business licenses*) of all segments of the ministry – the schools, the orphanages, the hospital, and the Para-medical clinic.

*Second*, they seized all passports and bank accounts. By taking these illegal actions, they financially handicapped the entire ministry. When they froze the bank accounts, they crushed the very backbone of the ministry. It immediately stopped the flow of resources which kept the orphans fed. Providing food to the orphans became a major challenge. Paying the salaries of thousands of employees within the ministry was impossible. Most of the employees could not remain without pay. They had families of their own to support.

When they cancelled the registrations for the schools, the timing was devastating for the ministry. The schools were in the midst of their annual academic examinations when they shut the entire school system down.

*Third*, they began proceedings to confiscate the ministry property. All this hatred poured out on a man – my father – who was both a faithful servant of God and an honored citizen of this country. Still, the courts – who knew my father's reputation - issued a decree that would permit the officials to confiscate all the ministry property. Their purpose was clearly to destroy what God had built over these past 50 years through Hopegivers International!

But God protects - in advance - what He deems must be protected. The government could not confiscate anything of my father's, because he did not personally own anything. The only thing I owned was an old motorcycle! The government officials were shocked when they learned that the founder and Chairman of Hopegivers International – which encompasses a lot of property – did not have one penny to his name. The police just don't get it. My father's treasure was always laid up in a place where neither the police or thieves or insects could reach it. He had stored up riches in heaven. He spent every day of his life storing up new wealth!

> *"But store up for yourselves treasures in heaven, where moth and rust do not destroy and where thieves do not break in and steal."*
> *Matthew 6:20-21*

After I was arrested, the police went into the orphanages and took all the files. The files would allow them to locate all of our pastors. To this day, they have not returned those files to the ministry. The religious fundamentalists broke in and took light fixtures, fans – anything of value that wasn't nailed down.

Once they crippled the ministry financially, the mobs took over and began to damage many of the properties in Kota. School buses were smashed and students were beaten. The orphans were told that the orphanages would be burned to the ground so they had better leave. There were several attempts to do just that. There was even a bomb thrown into one of our buildings, but the staff was successful in retrieving it before it exploded.

The school buildings in Ramganjmandi and in Beawar were severely damaged. One of the servants of God – Augustine George – was brutally beaten in the public market place. The only thing that saved his life was his wife's bravery when she threw herself across his unconscious body to block the kicks that were being delivered repeatedly on him. The religious fanatics had every intention of finishing him off. Where were the police?

In order to appease the mobs and the political leaders, the police would relentlessly question our staff along with the students at the Bible College. The harassment by local officials was so severe that many left the organization so they could escape the constant interrogation. Even Mr. R. S. Nair – who for 30 years was the administrator of our ministry in India - submitted his resignation once he was granted bail by the Supreme Court.

It was like watching a tornado come through and literally destroy everything in its path. For some time, it looked as if the enemy would only rest once he had completely destroyed the ministry. Unfortunately for him, the church continued to fast and pray during the relentless persecution; our God hears the faithful and fervent prayers of His people.

*"The prayer of a righteous man is powerful and effective." James 5:16*

After the news of my arrest spread, religious fundamentalist groups and other anti-Christian factions publicly demonstrated their approval by lighting fire-crackers. My potential demise gave them reason for loud celebration. Many of our religious friends separated themselves from us to insure their own safety. The smaller Christian groups were reportedly saying that they were "different" than Hopegivers. They didn't distribute Bibles or force conversions. Hopegivers does distribute Bibles, but we have never forced conversions!

While I was still in prison, I learned that the Social Welfare Minister – Mr. Madan Dilawar – intended to take over the orphanage where we housed 2400 children. The reason he gave for the takeover was because all of our bank accounts had been seized. We could not withdraw any money to feed the children. Unfortunately, if the children did not receive food due to lack of funds, they would die. The situation was becoming desperate very quickly.

We still do not know why Mr. Dilawar is against us. Neither my father nor I have ever had a confrontation or even a conversation with him. Politically, it is good for him to trouble the Christians. In his circle of influence, this strategy elevates his status. To this day, we do not hate him or wish him any harm. We simply want him to know the truth and speak the truth. The Bible says that the Lord prepares a table for us in the presence of our enemies. By this point in the persecution, our Hopegivers dining room table – prepared and monitored by the Lord - seated more that 10,000 enemies! Yet I know that the more enemies of the ministry, the more grace our Lord pours out on His children!

Prompted by purely selfish motives, Mr. Dilawar wanted to appear as the savior for the poor and oppressed by taking control of the orphanage. He actually did take control for a brief period. The orphanage was locked up and the police were guarding it. The Social Welfare Department had taken control while Mr. V.S. Thomas was under house arrest. Their management style was dictatorial and caused many of the children to run away from the orphanage out of fear. I was sick with worry over the children who had run away. Where would they run to? What was happening to them?

When I learned that he had taken control of the orphanage, I told anyone who would listen to me that I was going on a hunger strike if the Minister continued to control the orphanage.

When the orphans, who remained at the orphanage, heard of my decision they also threatened to go on a hunger strike. They refused to eat any food from the hands of the Minister. Those same children protested so loudly that they drove the Minister and his people out of the orphanage. He only had control – on and off – for 28 days before he finally gave up!

No, we did not go on a hunger strike. That was the last thing the police wanted to see happen. It would only draw attention to what the government and local police were doing to me and to the orphans. They could have cared less whether the orphans and I starved to death or not. They just didn't want mainline media to pick up the story – and they surely would have. They also didn't want me to be perceived as a martyr to the people. They know, as I do, that my death would only strengthen the resolve of thousands of Bible students and pastors all over India.

The government shut down our hospital and would not allow the employees to leave the premises. Sick patients who had been admitted to the hospital were asked to leave. Many children from the orphanages, who had been admitted to the hospital for various conditions, were sent away. The government appointed one of their doctors to oversee the staff.

The schools in various locations around Kota were all closed due to the lack of student registrations. The government told the public that all school registrations had been cancelled and that their children – even though they had already registered with our schools for the next session – would have to transfer to other schools. Consequently, we had to close three of our schools due to the decrease in student registrations. We lost 60-70 percent of our student enrollments due to forced transfers during this period. This of course promoted the other private schools in the city because they picked up all the kids that were told they had to transfer elsewhere. Some of these schools even helped to fund the persecution. The children that did stay on were the children of widows and lower caste families who had nowhere else to go. The wealthier families were the ones who took their children out of our schools.

By the time the High Court of Jaipur granted us interim bail – we had been in hiding from May, 2006 through August, 2006 – nearly everything had been ruined. Re-building the ministry was looking pretty overwhelming by this time.

# CHAPTER 9

**Bail**

The court refused to grant me permission to travel abroad and see my family. Although my wife, Shelley, did meet me briefly right after I was released from jail, she was forced to return to the United States without me. I thank God I have such a virtuous wife. She did not desert me even during the most trying times, and she continues to faithfully stand by me.

*"A wife of noble character who can find? She is worth far more than rubies.*
*Her husband has full confidence in her and lacks nothing of value. She brings him good, not harm, all the days of her life." Proverbs 31:10-12*

*"Give her the reward she has earned, and let her works bring her praise at*
*the city gate." Proverbs 31:30*

The High Court rejected my application to go abroad and see my family unless it was a special situation. How did they define a special situation? Someone in my family had to be critically ill or have died before permission would be granted for me to leave the country.

I was advised to prepare a fictitious paper saying that one of my family members was gravely ill, but then the Holy Spirit asked me, "Does God require the support of your false documentation to do His work?" I submitted to the leading of the Holy Spirit and decided to wait on God's timing. I knew that truth would eventually triumph. I continued to seek permission to leave and visit my family over the next 10 months. Each time the High Court refused my request.

The lawyer who was representing the government offered the argument that permission should only be granted if Samuel Thomas or Dr. M. A. Thomas required treatment abroad for cancer or some other grave sickness. When I heard these words from the advocate, I understood what Jesus meant when He said, "Bless them that curse you." I remember saying to the Lord, "Dear Lord, forgive this man because he does not know what he is saying." I knew that all who mock the people of God are meddling with the apple of His eye.

Finally, on March 21, 2007, the High Court turned our interim bail into regular bail. We thanked God for His intervention, and another prayer answered. In April of 2007, the High Court granted me permission to visit my wife and children in the states for 21 days (*which was actually only 18 days due to travel time*). So after 14 months of separation, I was able to be with my family. When I landed in the United States, Shelley and my two sons – Steven and Timothy – met me with tears of joy. Our hearts were so full of gratitude to a God that clearly delivered me from the very mouth of the lion.

The news of my arrival in the states spread like wildfire throughout the many churches who had been praying for our safety. When I shared my personal testimony - which I did everywhere I went in that month - I encouraged everyone to stand firm on the Word of God. I thanked them for all their prayers.

A few did ask me, "Brother Samuel, after all this humiliation and persecution, do you still want to remain in India and continue with this work?" I was able to answer with no hesitation, "*For me to live is Christ and to die is gain.*" Until the last drop of blood in my body is gone, my family and I will remain dedicated to fulfilling our mission to emancipate the citizens of our beloved India. We will do everything through Christ who strengthens us to rehabilitate and spiritually educate the people.

On April 28, 2007, after a wonderful time with my wife and sons, I arrived in India at the main office in Kota once again. I thanked God for all His goodness. But within 24 hours of my arrival, it became clear that the enemy was not finished with us. On May 2, the ministry vehicle was stolen from Jaipur with all the important documents we had gathered to present to the High Court in Jaipur the next day. This news was upsetting – to say the least. Without these documents, the judiciary process would be further delayed. We did not waste any of our precious time investigating who might have been behind the theft. We simply thanked God for

His continued presence, which would only
strengthen us through every additional trial.

Friends, we continue to experience one trial after
another, testing our perseverance to trust our God.
We refuse to give in to discouragement. I must
admit that this theft created a lot of inner turmoil for
me as well as for my lawyer. But in our quieter
moments, we know that Satan is behind it all in an
attempt to hinder our slow, but steady march toward
victory. I remember picking up my Bible during this
time with a very heavy heart. I opened it and my
eyes were immediately drawn to:

*"We are troubled on every side, yet not distressed;*
*we are perplexed, but not in despair; persecuted,*
*but not forsaken; cast down, but not destroyed;*
*always bearing about in the body the dying of the*
*Lord Jesus, that the life also of Jesus might be made*
*manifest in our body. For we who live are always*
*delivered unto death for Jesus' sake, that the life*
*also of Jesus might be made manifest in our mortal*
*flesh." 2 Corinthians 4:8-11*

# Chapter 10

## Life Today for Samuel, Shelley and Hopegivers International

### Question: Is the ministry still being actively persecuted today (2011)?

### Samuel:
*"Oh yes, the persecution continues. The accounts are still frozen, so getting money to the orphanages and paying employees is still a challenge each and every month. I am also in court monthly. The enemy continues to keep the hatred alive in the hearts of man and we have not been able to bring resolution to the false accusations.*

*"Twice since 2006, the documents that help prove my innocence were destroyed. The first time it happened, the rebels physically threw the driver and the riding attorney out of the vehicle and stole the jeep along with the lawyer's briefcase of documents. The second time the lawyer was eating in a restaurant when his jeep along with his briefcase and all its contents were stolen. Because the bank accounts remain frozen, I must be creative in order to raise the funds needed to feed the children. That's the only way we have been able to continue to care for the children day to day. When I am asked how I can continue to feed the children, I simply say, 'I get help from people.'*

*"Since 2006, I have had to shut down our 75 bed hospital to outside patients. Although all the equipment is still there, and we treat our staff and orphans in the facility, we have had to shut the doors to the general public. It has been closed since November of 2009. Our prayer is that things will turn around financially and we will once again be able to serve the community along with the orphans.*

*"The legal case against us now includes accusations concerning the map of India. There is a map – widely used on the Internet – that shows Kashmir faded out and as not being part of India. At one point that map was on a test web site. The offense only calls for a $50 fine, but because they want to jail me again, they have made a big deal out of it and turned the case into an anti-national/treason charge. So the cases against me remain open and ongoing. I must always schedule the trip to see my family around the many court appearances that are required of me.*

*"I am not praying for favor with the government in the court system. I am asking for boldness and clarity of mind when I am dealing with that system. If you look back over history, you will find that persecution always draws those being persecuted closer to God and brings others to a saving knowledge of Christ. I desire a very close walk with God on this earth.*

*"The persecution is a lesson to me and hopefully to others when I share our story with them. It has*

*taught me that we all need to believe more in the sovereignty of God. You see, God used the book* **Haqeeqat** *to put me where I am today spiritually. If you remember the story of Paul in the New Testament, Paul asked that a 'thorn' be removed from him. Just like Paul, I can't say for sure that God will ever remove the persecution from my life. I know that the Lord told Paul that His grace was sufficient. What I do know is that God will use the persecution in a way that will bring more souls into His Kingdom."*

**Shelley:**
*"As Samuel said, the persecution continues. Sometimes it feels as though there is no relief in sight. I never know from one visit to the next if I will see him again. I ask God regularly if He really means to trust me with so much. "* Laughing, she adds, *"But He did say that He would not give me more than I can handle. I guess you could say that the life we have been given is a vote of confidence in me from Him! Besides, I knew when Samuel proposed to me in 1986 that I was becoming part of something that was of eternal value."*

**Question: With the accounts still frozen, are you able to feed the orphans regularly?**

**Samuel:**
*"Yes, by God's grace, although it has become very difficult with the funds so low. Even the government had trouble feeding the kids 10 days in a row! The orphans are fed rice and lentils along with fresh vegetables three times a day. Meat is a rare treat for the orphans because the ministry cannot afford to feed them chicken or meat on a regular basis. The food is very good though in India. Our food tends to be consistently spicier than those in other countries. We season our vegetables with hot spices and then pour the seasoned vegetables over rice - a main staple in India. We are blessed to have many rice fields in India because the land in India is primarily agricultural."*

**Question: Do you miss living in India or are you afraid to go back because of the persecution your husband is going through?**

**Shelley:**
*"I did like living in India. When I first moved there after our wedding at age 19, I felt like I was in an Epcot Center 360 degree documentary, where everything was going on all around me and I was simply standing in the center watching. None of it seemed real to me at the time. But after a while, it no longer felt like a foreign country to me.*

*"When I moved back to the United States after living in India for 15 years in order to protect our*

*boys, it was a major adjustment for me. I had never lived alone. I moved from my parent's home to college dorms to a home in India, where we never lived alone – even as a family. My preference is to be where my husband and children are living. But until the boys are grown and off to college, I will remain in the states. Once the boys are grown, I hope to travel with my husband.*

*"I'm not afraid to go back to India. It's just not practical right now because I have the boys. I'm aware that they have also named me along with Samuel in the court case. They have labeled me as being anti-Indian/pro-Pakistani and an American spy. Go figure!"*

**Question: Samuel, how do you feel about Shelley and the boys living in the states so far away from you?**

**Samuel:**
*"I miss them very much and wish it could be different, but it isn't right now. I am so grateful to Shelley and the boys that they have chosen to support me and the ministry. Besides, since Shelley is named as a spy for the American government, I have peace knowing that she and the boys are safely away from all the lies and deception.*

*"Scripture tells us that we should always be wise as serpents and gentle as doves. I will always be*

*grateful for the wisdom given to me by my father
and the Board members of Hopegivers International
when they recommended that Shelley and the boys
be brought back to the states in 2001.*

*"In 2008, Steven – my oldest son – traveled back to
India with my Dad to spend two months with us. It
was definitely a more stressful time for me. I needed
to keep a watchful eye over a teenage boy without
neglecting all my other responsibilities. Teenagers
are not the easiest age group to keep watch over.
They don't have the same sense of danger as most
adults and are far too trusting. As soon as the cases
are cleared though, I am hoping that my family will
be able to come for Christmas each year."*

**Question: Is there any one thing that has
permanently changed you because of the
persecution?**

**Samuel:**
*"Yes. I have learned a lot about forgiveness over
these past five years. Less than 2 months ago, the
very man who held a gun to my head on March 17,
2006 and pulled the trigger – although it did not
discharge - came to see me at my office in Kota. He
told me that ever since that day, he hasn't been able
to sleep. He also lost a son in the months that
followed my capture and arrest. He placed both of
his guns on the table in front of me and asked my
forgiveness for his participation in the arrest -
especially for his desire and attempt to murder*

*me.*

*"In the past few months, some of the smaller Christian groups, who distanced themselves from us during the heat of the persecution, came to me and asked for my forgiveness. You see, I have no enemies since prison. My heart has changed forever. The Holy Spirit changed my heart in a way that prevents me from seeing any man as my enemy."*

## Question: Do you work in the ministry as well?

**Shelley:**
*"A few years ago I worked in the ministry office full time. I answered phones and email correspondence, kept Samuel's speaking schedule, and organized the schedules of American volunteer teams that traveled to India. But the boys began to resent the time I spent away from them. It was a little different those first few years we were in the states; we actually ran the ministry out of two rooms in the guest house where we lived initially. Now that our home and the ministry office are in two separate locations, I am not as active in the day-to-day management of the ministry as I once was. I do still work with volunteers who go on short term mission trips to India. I communicate how projects supported by US donors – like wells, churches, schools and Hope Homes – are progressing. Although I have some busy days, my responsibilities keep me freed up so that I can be there for the boys.*

*Being teenagers, they keep me running. Between homework, projects, baseball, basketball, guitar lessons, school and church, one of them has me transporting them somewhere nearly every night of the week."*

**Question: How do you keep the marriage together?**

**Samuel:**
*"It's all about God's grace and provision. It's not any fun being away from Shelley and the boys, but I can't change what God has assigned me to do. I just ask Him to protect my family and give us all peace. As much as possible, I call every day to check in with Shelley, to hear her voice and let her know how much I love her and the boys. While I was in prison, I was comforted by the fact that if something happened to me, at least Shelley and the boys have a home fully paid for due to the generosity of a donor. They would not be out on the street should I actually be put to death.*

*"If it is for the sake of the Gospel, I will go to prison if that's what the courts decide. I want to die a martyr's death because I know that the blood of martyrs is the seed of the church. What honor is there in dying of cancer or in a car accident? I want to die one day for the cause of Christ!*
*"Do I want to go back to prison? Absolutely not, but if the sovereign will of God says I must go, then*

*I will go. It is said that prayer changes things, but I believe that prayer mostly changes us! I am calmer, more trusting of God and His provision for my family since my prison experience."*

**Shelley:**
*"This is the life God has given us. There is no such thing as an ordinary life in ministry whether you pastor a church or you work on the mission field. If I complained or nagged, it wouldn't make anything better. It would simply make our precious times together as a couple miserable. God knows what He is doing and we are both certain that we are right in the center of His will.*

*"Regardless of what other people might think, Samuel is not choosing his work over me and the boys. If other people think that about him, then perhaps more people should step up to the plate and help in the ministry so my husband can spend more time at home.*

*"I also have a passion for the ministry – I just do it differently. I have my part to play and Samuel has his. What I do best is pray for the ministry, for my husband and then of course, care for our boys."*

**Question: What will happen to the ministry if they do put you back in prison? Since your father passed away, who will take over the leadership duties if something happens to you?**

**Samuel:**

*"This is God's ministry, so I don't understand why people worry about the ministry falling apart if I die or go to prison? God will give me and our partners the wisdom to expand the leadership or replace me when the time comes. I would love it if one of my sons had a desire to minister to the orphans, but their life path must also be one that God gives them and not one their father wishes for them. You see, I don't see myself as helping God; I'm just doing what He wants me to do. As long as any of us will make the effort to look beyond ourselves, we will always find ourselves in the center of God's will.*

*"I am told by the accountants that we need 40 million dollars each year to support this ministry. We have never raised more than 1.5 million dollars. Yet not one of our children has gone hungry. How do I explain that? **I can't**! If I could explain how a miracle takes place in this ministry year after year, then it would not have been God who did it. Surely God is caring for these children. The Lord calls us to be prudent and wise, but I believe that when we focus too much on the business aspect of anything, we are usually spending a lot of effort on self. If Jesus is not the Lord of all, then He is not the Lord of anything! I am convinced that we need not get worked up over anything we have no control over. Those are definitely the things we must leave up to God! The Lord will bless those who care for*

*the orphans and widows. We trust Him to do just
that."*

**Question: Is Samuel different here in the states
then when you lived in India as a family?**

**Shelley:**
*"There is always a lot of activity around Samuel,
whether he is in India or in the states. He rests
better when he is here and we definitely have much
more time together as a family then we did when we
lived in India. In India, there were always guests in
the house, and every meal was shared with other
people.*

*"When Sam is here for a few weeks he likes to clean
and polish the cars, rearrange the furniture and
clean out closets."* She laughs, *"The
rearrangements drive me to distraction, but I know
that it is simply a stress reducer for him. When he
does some of these "more homey" things, he gets to
see the end result. In ministry, things are never
finished. There are always more abandoned and at-
risk children to be rescued, fed, sheltered and
educated. The tasks are never completed.*

*"He will spend time bouncing ideas off me and
always has a long list of stuff to buy and take back
with him. The house is in disorder for a week after
he leaves. He's on speaking tours from Saturday
afternoon until Monday morning. These are very
necessary, but I can't help but pray for more*

*speaking engagements closer to home so he can be at home more on the weekends when the boys aren't in school.*

*"I would like to be more like Samuel. He sees humor in so many circumstances; he laughs easily. Samuel is great at not letting stressful situations get him down. I try to keep in mind that we are all, after all, only human and sanctification happens to be a life-long process.*

*"Until he was arrested, I wasn't conscious of a little habit I began after we moved to the states. I would always leave at least one shirt of Samuel's unlaundered until his next trip home. That way I always have something that smells like him. Even today, I never know when I might see him again. When he's in India, I don't tell him about every annoyance I deal with while raising two boys alone. There's nothing he can do for us from India anyway. Besides, he just doesn't need the additional stress.*

*"Samuel is more of a disciplinarian than I am. I don't have a highly structured temperament, so I tend to pick my battles with the boys as they grow older. But with Samuel, they jump when he says jump. The more frequent Samuel's visits to the states, the better the boys behave when he is gone. It's more of an adjustment after Samuel leaves to go back to India for me. While he's here, he takes on half of the parenting responsibilities. Once he*

*leaves, it all falls back on my shoulders. But I know my husband's heart, and he would be with us if he could."*

**Question: What was life like for you and your father after he suffered the stroke in 2008? I'm sure caring for him along with all the other responsibilities of running a ministry had to be difficult for you.**

**Samuel:**
*"Dad had good days and he had bad days. He never recovered the ability to speak or read and was bound to a wheel chair until the day he died in 2010. He understood everything you said to him, and he prayed continuously. We made sure – when he was feeling well enough – to take him to the orphanage and to church so he could listen to and watch the children praise God. Our God is sovereign and He had His reasons for not healing my Dad."*

He laughs, *"People don't always like what I have to say when I bring a message concerning the sovereignty of God. It's not my most popular message, but then I'm not running for election either. We need to learn to let God be God. My Dad was very sick. God had a reason for allowing that sickness and why He didn't take him home to heaven sooner. I know that God knew what I wanted. That was, and still is enough for me.*

*"When everything is going well for us, we tend not to lean on God's understanding. But God does not use anyone greatly until He hurts them deeply. Let me give you an every day example of what I mean by that.*

*"Let's say you have a broken coffee mug. Will you deliberately pull that mug out of your cupboard to serve a guest? No! You want to serve your guest with the finest you have in your cupboard. Although that may be your kitchen, it's not God's kitchen. He only uses broken vessels – vessels whose brokenness have made them stronger by God's glue – the presence of His Holy Spirit.*

*"Before Dad had his stroke, I took care of all the administrative duties. Dad led most of the prayer meetings, encouraged the pastors, and ran the evangelical meetings. Now I do all of that along with the administrative work. Yes, it was and is harder, but necessary. "*

**Question: I understand that there have been several assassination attempts on you and your father's life. How do you feel about that?**

**Samuel:**
*"Well, I don't like it, of course!"* He laughs. *"We have had several close calls when it comes to assassination attempts – both on my father and me. My Dad used to say, 'Look, if God can use two*

*dummies like me and Samuel, He can do far more without us!'*

*"It was a privilege to serve with my father. We fought wars together – my Dad and I. I had a great relationship with him. One day I want to write a book entitled - **A Father and Son**."*

**Question: Did your father – Dr. M. A. Thomas – become angry with God over his physical condition?**

**Samuel:**
*"No. He was never angry with God, and he did not complain either. He did however sometimes sit and cry, because he couldn't do much to grow the ministry. That's why I took him with me whenever I could, and whenever he was physically able. I never left him behind, and I told him I would never leave him behind. One day a visitor said to me in front of him, 'Oh, what a burden it must be to care for your father in his condition.' I replied to that man, looking straight at my father. 'It is my privilege to care for my father. He is like the Ark of the Covenant to me. Where he is, there will be blessings.' My dad had tears in his eyes. I then said to him. 'It doesn't matter if God heals you or not, as long as the Lord keeps you here on earth, it is my privilege to care for you as you have cared for so many orphans, widows and outcasts. From my perspective, it is such a small thing that I do for you. I am proud to be your son.'"*

**Question: Still, it must be very stressful when the funds needed to run the ministry don't come in as expected.**

**Samuel:**
He laughs, *"Yes, there is plenty of stress to go around. But when I recall the story about the young lad in John 6, I can't remain discouraged. You see, the boy only had 5 loaves of bread and 2 fish, but he brought the little he had to the Lord. There is a lot stress when the money does not look as though it will do what is necessary to keep the orphans fed, but the Lord knows our needs. He also wants us to know that He is in control.*

*"I believe that the Lord has a solution planned before we even know we have a problem! It's a beautiful privilege to trust in the Lord. He expects us to come with our solution - like the boy who brought his few fish and pieces of bread when there were over 5,000 men, women and children to feed. He is looking for trusting servants. He not only fed the multitude, but there were 12 baskets of food left over. He gives to each of us more than we can possibly imagine, but He gives in His way and in His time!*

*"You see, God doesn't need Samuel; I need God. His eye is on the sparrow – so if He's watching one little sparrow, you and I can be certain that His eye is on us. And if He is watching us that closely, there is no need to be afraid or discouraged!*

*"When I was a very young man, I wanted to become a medical doctor. But when the time came to make a career choice, I realized that God didn't need just my money. He wanted my life. You see, I once thought that if I could become a doctor, I could pour lots of money into the ministry and help the orphans. But God had other plans for my life and I had to follow His will; not mine.*

*"People ask me, 'Why should I visit the Hopegivers ministry in India? I can just give the money and you could do so much more.' That sounds like a logical and practical solution, but if the Lord has put it on your heart to go on a short-term mission trip to India, or anywhere else in the world, it is probably because He has something that He wants to do in your life. Once you see what He is doing in the lives of people around the world, you will want to be involved at every level and the Lord will bless you and use you even more. He is beyond local and national, our God is global.*

*"In Acts 1:8 we are commanded to go and witness in all places. No ministry would be lacking funds if everyone who said they would give instead of going on a mission trip actually did give! When we don't follow through with giving, it is usually due to one of those Christian excuses like: 'I will pray about it.'*

*"Here's the thing I would like to propose. Why not ask the Lord whether He wants you to give or if He wants you to go to the mission field. If He says*

*neither, then you call me and let me know.*
*Otherwise, do whatever He asks of you!"*


**Question: Do you ever get down or depressed
and want to quit?**

**Samuel:**
*"I must be honest. I have been on the edge of
quitting several times – probably like anyone
else would be when the pressures are many and
very strong. When I find myself in that place,
I stop working. I will take time off for a few hours
and spend that time recounting all the victories
we've had in the ministry. Once I feel more
refreshed, I go back to work.*

*"I also don't like to talk with others about my
problems. I have found that over the years, if
I talk to another person about the challenges I am
facing, it only makes it harder for me to
persevere without wallowing around in some self-
pity issues. I go to God! He did tell us that
we are to take all our burdens to Him, and I take
this word literally. He also said;*

*"Let us not become weary in doing good, for at the
proper time we will reap a harvest if we do not
give up." Galatians 6:9*

*"It's important that we all be doers of the Word –
not just readers. I like to tell people that a*

*genuine leather Bible needs a Christian with good leather shoes!"*

*"Do not merely listen to the Word, and so deceive yourselves. Do what it says!" James 1:22*

**Question: I've read several times about the ministry's goal to develop ONE MILLION ARROWS/churches. Why one million?**

**Samuel:**
*"We set a goal of 1 million because M. A. Thomas and Samuel Thomas might be able to establish some lesser number of churches in their own strength. We chose a number that cannot be done in our own strength! Only God can establish **ONE MILLION ARROWS** through this ministry. We want to be very clear about who gets the credit here. It is not M. A. or Samuel. We serve an awesome God who works miracles! People will soon forget my Dad's testimonies and mine, but they won't forget Scripture and God's manifestation of His promises through ordinary men. Unless God pours His strength into us, we can't accomplish the really big dreams. But we can do all things through Him who strengthens us!"*

**Question: Have you and Samuel been able to get away together since he was released from prison?**

**Shelley:**

*"All time we spend together is special for us, but some dear friends did send us on a week long trip in the summer of 2009. We'd never had that kind of time together in the 23 years that we have been married."* She laughs, *"It was such a sweet treat. We enjoyed the time to be together and talk and even be silent together. But we also allowed each other our alone times as well. Ministry has taught us to be very accepting of each other's needs and temperaments."*

**Question: Is there anything else you would like to add before we end this interview Dr. Samuel?**

**Samuel:**

*"Yes, thank you for asking. In the book of Genesis, Chapter 22, I believe there is a relevant message for those of us living in the 21st century. We must learn – as Abraham did – that the safest place for our "Isaac" is on the altar of God. Today, our Isaac might be our children, bank accounts, careers, or even our reputations. Our Isaac can be many and varied in these modern times.*

*"The story of Abraham and Isaac – although it was definitely a dress rehearsal for Calvary – has a practical message for each of us. If you remember the story, Abraham continued to reassure his son, Isaac, that God would provide the sacrifice once it was time for it to be offered. Abraham didn't have any idea how God would care*

*for his Isaac, but he had faith that He would - even*
*as he placed his son up on the altar.*

*"You see, the safest place for the Isaac in our lives*
*is on the altar – handing it completely over*
*to the care of God. This is why I know that*
*Hopegivers International will remain fruitful*
*long after M. A. Thomas and Samuel Thomas are*
*gone. We place this ministry on God's altar*
*every single day. There are days when it is certainly*
*more difficult than others, but we put it up there*
*anyway. The ministry belongs to God and He will*
*care for it in His way and fulfill His purpose and in*
*His timing. I'm convinced of it!"*

# Hopegivers International "Rope Holders"*

How can you partner with Hopegivers International? It starts with a heart that longs to offer oneself as a "rope holder" for those who lay their lives down on the mission fields.

*"Let each one do just as he has purposed in his heart; not grudgingly or under compulsion; for God loves a cheerful giver." 2 Corinthians 9:7*

This book was written to bring glory to God and to introduce "a cheerful giver" to a way in which he or she can further the Gospel in the 10/40 window. If the Lord is speaking to your heart about partnering with Hopegivers as we gather **ONE MILLION ARROWS** for the cause of Christ, please contact us so you too can grab hold of the rope that is spiritually tied to thousands of pioneer missionaries who live and preach in some of the darkest corners, spiritually speaking, of the earth. We are publishing this book in order to give hearts – already prepared by God - a chance to grab hold of that rope and contribute financially or in any other way the Lord leads them.

Too often congregations, families and even individuals are stirred out of guilt to open their pocket books in order to fill a need. It happens when your local fire department calls or when your pastor collects money for missions once a month.

Unfortunately, guilt is quite volatile. It evaporates sometimes even before the check is written!

At Hopegivers we do not want guilt-driven donors; we want God-driven donors! If someone else can talk you into working with the ministry, then someone can also talk you out of it. But when God moves on your heart to be involved in one of His missions, we are assured that no one can talk you out of it. For confirmation, just go to the Old Testament. When God gave Moses the command to build the Ark of the Covenant, listen to where He said the material to build it would come from:

*"...take from among you a contribution to the Lord; whoever is of a willing heart"...*
*Exodus 35:5*

*"And everyone whose heart stirred him and everyone whose spirit moved him came and brought the Lord's contribution for the work..."*
*Exodus 35:21*

We are unique at Hopegivers. Although we gather, sharpen and launch the native Indians as pioneer missionaries throughout India and other parts of the world, we are not just about the nationals, the indigenous or even native missionaries. We invite anyone who has a gift or talent they want to contribute for the work of the Lord to come along side us as we work toward establishing **ONE MILLION ARROWS** for the cause of Christ. If you have been blessed financially – then send your blessings in so we can take in more children and train more missionary pastors. If you have been blessed with the gift of wisdom, teaching or preaching, then please come and help us train our young men as pastors. Better yet, use your gifts to share about Hopegivers International in your local churches and within your home communities! The rewards are the same – always eternal in nature – regardless of the gift or talent you share. What matters is that you bring that gift to Jesus and allow Him to multiply it beyond your wildest dreams!

When the Lord moves on a heart, we gain a ministry partner for life; one who prays for the ministry; one who remains faithful to help us build the Kingdom of God here on earth with orphaned and abandoned children – children who also have a passion to spread the Gospel to parts of the world where the name of Jesus has never been spoken.

We are *not* in the "heart moving" business; that's the Holy Spirit's territory. We are in the business of collecting fragments (*children no one else wants or cares about*). We feed them, shelter them, educate them and share the love of God with them so they are equipped to one day re-enter their community as productive and godly influences. You and I are the "bow"; the children are the "arrows"; God is the "quiver". Our "targets" are unsaved souls who have never heard the Good News!

This book is being distributed to every corner of the world where God has blessed a country with believers who have a passion for reaching the lost and forgotten with the Gospel of Jesus Christ. We are in the business of connecting Kingdom people here in the states with Kingdom people in India and every other corner of the earth that is waiting to hear about our Savior. Our goal is to enlarge God's Kingdom boundaries and therefore accomplish the Great Commission – regardless of the ocean between us. Won't you join us?

*William Carey, English missionary to India (1793-1834, who coined the phrase "Rope Holders" in the 1800's)*

# Other Assaults on God's People

**Since 2005**:

Religious fundamentalists, committed to protecting the uniqueness of their religion by using violence, target our ministries constantly. It does not matter where in India our pastors and orphanages are located; they want to abolish all of them.

There has been persecution since Dr. M. A. Thomas began the ministry over 50 years ago. Many have been martyred and many more beaten and even permanently maimed for the cause of Christ. We wanted to share a few of many that have taken place just since 2005.

*"For we do not wrestle against flesh and blood, but against principalities, against powers, against the rulers of the darkness of this age, against spiritual hosts of wickedness in the heavenly places."*
*Ephesians 6:12*

## Pastor Mangilal Moosa:

In 2005, nearly 6000 Bible students graduated and were sent out to various parts of the country to minister the Gospel of Jesus Christ. In February of 2006, another 10,000 Bible students completed their courses and were sent into

the mission field. The anti-Christians were enraged over the ever-expanding ministry. When they learned of the large graduation ceremony scheduled for February, 2006 their hatred assailed the ministry on all sides. They were determined that the graduation would not take place. Although Hopegivers cancelled the graduation services and moved it a long distance away from Kota, we still experienced brutal attacks. They just took place in other parts of India.

Pastor Mangilal Moosa is serving God in a small village called Tindore in North India. In the very frigid month of December, 2005 he entered the freezing waters of a river and baptized 150 people. These were people who sought out and found the truth of Christ in the last few years. They chose to be baptized and remain true to God despite persecution. The news of the baptisms reached the ears of local anti-Christians. They joined forces to protest the baptisms. They did not carry out their threats during the larger gatherings of believers though.

They began a campaign of threats targeting Pastor Mangilal Moosa. They tried every means at their disposal to scare him away from the village, but Pastor Moosa stood firm. They had the pastor watched constantly in hopes of catching him in some illegal act so they could throw him into prison. During this period of surveillance, a 6 month old baby died of jaundice in a village 15 kilometers from Tindore – Mangilal's village. Hearing of the baby's death, the anti-Christian group plotted to turn a case of natural death into a homicide so they could implicate the pastor and his colleagues in the baby's death. As suspects for murder, their hope was that the pastor would be thrown in jail.

This heartless group of men dug up the infant's body and literally pummeled the body of the baby girl using thick wooden sticks. They smashed her ribs and then took the baby to a doctor who was asked to perform an autopsy. They then re-buried the child. Once the baby was buried, these men went to the police station and filed a false report of homicide against Mangilal and his co-workers. They also linked another man in the lawsuit who supplied provisions for the orphanage. Ten people were accused of murder. When the incident occurred and the arrest warrants were issued, Pastor Mangilal was not even in his native village. He had travelled to another village that was a day and a night's journey by road in order to preach the Gospel. He was completely out of the area while this conspiracy was being carried out and he had no idea what was happening at home as he ministered elsewhere.

As soon as the FIR (*First Information Report*) was issued, the police went into action and arrested nine of the accused. Because the police believed that these men were guilty of this heinous crime, they punched and battered each of them before throwing them into a prison cell. Before the police beat them, the accusing anti-Christian mob ruthlessly assaulted them.

The villagers were justifiably frightened as they witnessed this mass beating. It seemed that the church would suffer severely due to the violence stirred up by the enemy. The police and the mob were now looking for Pastor Mangilal Moosa. Once the pastor was informed of what was taking place in his village, he knew that it was all a scheme by the anti-Christians. He also knew that if he fell into their hands, they would beat him to death. If that happened, the innocent people in the village would never learn the truth. He decided that wisdom dictated it would be wise flee and go into hiding just as Elijah did when he hid from Jezebel and Ahab. Just because we are willing to be martyrs doesn't mean that we should offer ourselves up as a sacrifice.

When the enemy realized that Mangilal had escaped, they were infuriated and increased the pressure on the police to hunt him down and arrest him. The nine who had already been arrested and put into custody were told, "You will be released on bail only when Mangilal surrenders. Otherwise, you will rot in jail." The families of these nine innocent men were beside themselves. They were already impoverished financially and now they were mentally broken. Things looked hopeless. Their only resort was in tearful prayers.

When Pastor Mangilal learned of his co-workers plight, he decided to surrender. On January 22, 2006 he set out to turn himself into the police. But on the way to turn himself in, he was attacked by the anti-Christian mob. They dragged him into the police station only after hitting and kicking him viciously. By the time the police got him, his clothes were torn and his body was bruised and bleeding. He had multiple internal injuries and his body was swollen from all the abuse. Like his co-workers, the police then railed on his bloodied body with blows and kicks.

At night they would tie his legs together at the ankles and hang him upside down from a tree. As he hung from the tree, the police would take turns beating him with rods on the soles of his feet, legs, hands, and back. When one man tired of beating him, he'd go rest and another would take his place to continue the beatings. While beating him, they would abuse him verbally as well. Poor Mangilal! He was a simple preacher of the truth and a believer in love and goodness. He was a guide to the blind and a light to those walking in the darkness; a defender of the oppressed and needy. Broken, both physically and mentally, he assumed that the beatings and constant torture would eventually claim his life. Yet, in spite of his physical pain, his heart was full of joy because he knew this truth.

*"For me to live is Christ and to die is gain."*
*Philippians 1: 21*

While beating him, the police would threaten him saying, "Mangilal, if you want to survive, you must not turn any more people into Christians. If you will deny your Jesus Christ now, you will escape." A religious fundamentalist brought an idol of a goddess and said, "Bow down before this goddess." Mangilal refused to bow before the idol. His refusal earned him more blows. They were also delivering the same abuse to the other nine co-workers. They also refused to bow down to the lifeless image and were cruelly beaten. The more they were beaten, the more firmly they held to their faith in the living Lord, Jesus Christ. Being of one mind, they boldly told the police, "We are not only ready to be beaten; we are also ready to die for Jesus. We know where we will go after our death. We do not want to become cursed and go to hell after denying our Lord Jesus. It is better to suffer for Christ and reign with Him forever."

Mangilal was detained in police custody for 29 days. Every night during those 29 days they would wake him and beat him mercilessly. They would even cut him with razor blades. Even though he was locked up in the police station, the anti-Christians could walk in everyday and beat him up. They were a determined group with one demand, "Deny Jesus Christ, and you will be allowed to live." They would repeat these words over and over as they hit and kicked him.

Unfortunately, the police in this village looked at Mangilal and his nine colleagues through the tinted glasses of religious prejudice. These men were supposed to be socially responsible, but they were not interested in the truth of the charges levied against them. They too had only one purpose – to shatter the faith of these men. But thanks to the judiciary court that does not look through the same tinted glass, relief was in sight.

After one and a half months of detention, the court issued orders for the release of Mangilal's nine co-workers on bail. But due to the pressure placed on the political leaders by the leader of the religious fundamentalist group, an order was issued that Mangilal should not be granted bail. He was to be given the severest form of punishment. They wanted him to die rather than be released.

During his 1 year imprisonment, Mangilal watched as 22 of the inmates died. Satan had almost convinced him that he too would die in jail. But God's promises filled his thoughts and they continued to give him hope.

*"Do not fear, for I am with you. Only believe."*

The soles of his feet and his body stayed black and blue because of the constant beatings. It became difficult for him to go to the toilet. He was assigned to clean the toilets daily. He had to sweep and carry the waste away every day; he had to do this in spite of his already broken body or they would beat him again.

They would frequently come to his cell and beat him for some silly reason. Often, other inmates who were religious fundamentalists would hide razor blades under his blankets while he was working somewhere in the jail. The police would periodically search the cells and when they found razor blades in Mangilal's cell, he would be beaten and cut with the razors.

In spite of all these troubles, he tried to put on a cheerful face. It was his daily practice to teach the Bible and pray for everyone. Other inmates became attracted to him because of his attitude in prison. Some sympathized with him and would listen to him speak about his Lord. The Lord gave him the opportunity to preach the Gospel to 800 prisoners. The Lord's desire and command for all of us is to:

*"Preach the Gospel. Be ready in season and out of season. Endure afflictions, do the work of an evangelist, and do the full work of the ministry."*
*2 Timothy 4:5*

Ten inmates believed in the Good News proclaimed by Mangilal and received Jesus Christ as their personal Savior. They promised Mangilal that as soon as they were released from prison, they would be baptized and publicly proclaim to the world that they had transformed hearts. They gave Mangilal the addresses of their families and requested that he visit them when he was released. They wanted their families to also hear the Good News of salvation. Today, these families all attend Mangilal's church.

In spite of the torture and the bad food in prison, Mangilal gained weight - 10 kgs. This has to be a miracle. God cares for His children even under impossible conditions. *Proverbs 3:7-8* says:

*"Be not wise in thine own eyes: fear the Lord and depart from evil. It shall be health to thy navel and marrow to thy bones."*

Many people tried to get Mangilal released on bail, but the court always refused. There seemed to be no end to the heartbreaks. His wife and children were in a desperate condition financially and emotionally. The days were living nightmares, yet they too hung onto their faith. They knew only one thing - they were:

*"To participate in God's purpose, because they are fellow-laborers with God in the work of the Gospel." Philippians 4: 3*

Homicide cases carry a punishment of either life in prison or the death penalty. Finally, witnesses on behalf of the public prosecution were brought in to testify. Not one of them was willing to falsely accuse these men. It is written in the Bible:

*"The ungodly shall not stand in judgment."*
*Psalm 1:5*

The doctor who had done the autopsy was called in to testify. He said, "It is true that the ribs of this infant were fractured, but the child died before its ribs were broken." On January 20, 2007 Mangilal and the other nine servants of God were found not guilty. On January 22, 2007 Mangilal walked out of the jail. Praise the Lord!

At this time, the Word of God is being spread throughout Tindore and the other neighboring villages. In January of 2006, while Mangilal was still in jail, 27 more people were baptized. The blood of God's servants is never shed in vain. Each drop is a seed that mushrooms and spreads the Gospel throughout the world.

## Bishop Paulose

 The persecution in the last few years by the anti-Christian religious fundamentalists is not limited to Rajasthan alone. It has spread into other territories as well. It has become a regular hobby of our enemies to find, beat, mock, falsely accuse and jail any servants of God working in the nation of India. The acts of terror have become so violent that we have had times when the Bible teachers and students in the seminary located in Kota have had to flee overnight. A large number of our Bible Institutes are in Andhra Pradesh. That is why the February, 2006 graduation was done in Anathpur, in Andhra Pradesh, under the supervision of Bishop O.

Paulose. Even Bishop Paulose has been targeted by the anti-Christians.

A false case was filed against him and he was beaten and jailed twice.

## Pastor Jeremiah Mazee

In the state of Orissa, Pastor Jeremiah Mazee was serving the Lord. When he baptized nine people, the religious fundamentalists decided to file a false case of criminal offense against him as well. They accused him of smuggling drugs and other narcotic substances. The irony of this accusation is that this pastor was so poor that he lived in a hut. He couldn't even afford a chair or a bed in his hut. He didn't own a cycle – so he had no method of transportation.

Even the District Magistrate declared the charges against Jeremiah unsubstantiated. Besides, he was aware that the religious fundamentalists never brought charges against the real criminals of society. When the District Magistrate voiced his reservations regarding the implausible charges of smuggling against Jeremiah, the fundamentalists threatened him. If he wanted to remain in his political seat, then he had better keep his mouth shut. Afraid, he became silent, and Jeremiah was put in jail. Once he was jailed, they burned down his hut. After a year and a half, he was released.

When he came to the Pastor's Conference in October, 2008 he challenged the Bible College students. "If I die in that village, is there anyone who will take my place?" Five students stood up and volunteered, knowing what would be facing them. The pastors and students raised enough funds to rebuild his hut and to buy him a motorcycle.

## Dr. Dennis Nathaniel

 "On Feb 16, 2006 while preparing to preach at a conference that morning, I received a cell phone call. It was the police inspector from Kota informing me that he was at my home and he wanted me to come there immediately. I later learned that the police inspector and three constables had not only entered my home, but had brought 25 local police officers with them who surrounded it. They confronted my son and pregnant daughter-in-law as to my whereabouts.

"In my country, the only time police ever come to your home and surround it is if you are suspected of being a criminal. I am not a criminal, but now my neighbors are beginning to believe that I might be. The police inspector said that if I didn't come immediately, they would arrest my son instead.

"I told him to leave my home immediately. I would meet him at the local police station as soon as I hung up. I was only 10 kilometers from my home at the time.

"I cannot tell you how surprised I was at what was taking place. What could I have possibly done to warrant such treatment? The police inspector and the constables had driven several hours from Kota to arrest me! The 25 police officers who accompanied them were local to my area.

"They picked me up at the local police station and we drove eight hours back to Kota where I was put into police custody at Kota Central Jail. They are not allowed to keep a suspected terrorist – my supposed crime - beyond 14 days. It was a miserable 14 days! Although I was allowed to use a toilet, I was not allowed to bathe during those 14 days. I was arrested during a hot season, so you can just imagine the condition of my body after 14 days.

"At the end of 14 days they took me to the Kota jail where I was placed into judicial custody. I remained in that jail for four months until bail was finally granted to me by the High Court. Mr. V. S. Thomas, Director of the Kripa Orphanage, was arrested the same day as me. He was the first of our small group to be granted temporary bail. Samuel was next and then finally I was granted bail.

"During those four months I worried as much about my wife as I did myself. I shed many tears and experienced much fear during those days. My fears were primarily over money. My family does not have money – we are very poor. The only income we have comes through me. I did not know how my wife would purchase food, or get money for an advocate since I was now in jail. She could not even come to see me by train because there was no money for a ticket. Shortly after Dr. Samuel received bail, he had to go back into hiding, so even he didn't know my situation. My only crime was translating the book **Haqeeqat** from English into Hindi!

"During the four months I was imprisoned, my health, specifically my arthritis, deteriorated. I lost 14 pounds during those months. Without access to any medication, the pain in my body was nearly unbearable. I am so grateful to Dr. Samuel Thomas for helping me with medication since being released from jail. It allows me to be productive in my ministry.

"After Samuel was released on bail and I was left alone in the jail, I became despondent. The loneliness was overwhelming. There was no news from the outside, so I had no idea what was going on. I felt very alone. I didn't know if I would ever be released on bail. The only way anyone could visit me was to bribe the guards. Unfortunately, no one had any money at this time. All of the ministry accounts had been frozen by government officials. It wasn't long before I found myself considering suicide.

"I remember as if it were yesterday; it was May 13, 2006. I was lying on my cot using my Bible for a pillow. Because of the mosquitoes, rats and cockroaches, sleep was nearly impossible in jail. But for some reason, I actually fell sound asleep that day for the first time since being arrested. I was awakened suddenly by a loud voice. Startled, I lifted my head just as the ceiling fan - 16 feet in the air above my cot - fell to the ground. It missed my head by the width of two fingers. If not for the voice that awakened me a second before the fan came hurling to the ground, I would have been killed. It was 4 am in the morning. As I sat there in shock over such a close brush with death, I knew in my heart that God did not want me to commit suicide. He had other plans for my life.

"Because there were cameras on us 24/7, the guards watching the monitors saw the fan fall. That is when they decided to move me into a cell with 52 other prisoners. None of the prisoners liked me. They thought that Dr. Samuel and Dr. M. A. Thomas had insulted their gods and goddesses – the lie being propagated by the media. But after 15 days of talking with them and sharing the Gospel, all of them became my friends!

"It was also during this period that my arthritic pain became severe. At one point, the pain was so excruciating that I could not even lift my arms to feed myself or take in a cup of water. These prisoners, now my friends, would feed me and give me water. Praise God for how He can touch hearts so His children are cared for.

"During this month alone in the jail, away from my friends, the Lord gave me many Bible verses that I claimed as my own. It was during this time that I learned the practical application of the Word of God to my life. My wife, also a Christian, learned a lot about the power of prayer.

"My prison experience strengthened me spiritually. I do not believe that anything or anyone can shake my faith. I may not be healthy physically, but I am spiritually healthy. I continue to grow in the Lord every day. I now can see how that extra month in jail was simply an opportunity to preach the Gospel to 52 men who would not have heard it otherwise."

## Anthony Soren

In Jharkhand, Pastor Anthony Soren is serving God among several tribal groups. He oversees 10 churches and a Hope Home for orphaned and abandoned children. There were 51 children in the home.

When the bank accounts of the ministry were frozen in March of 2006, all of the orphanages faced financial challenges. With no money coming in, they had great difficulty in providing food and other necessities for the children. While I was in the Kota jail, we had no choice but to close down the orphanages. The office sent word to Anthony Soren that we had no way to fund his orphanage until we could resolve all the legal problems as a result of my arrest. We told him that we would send provisions once a verdict was passed concerning the false accusations.

What was Anthony going to do to protect these 51 orphans? Their lives were literally at stake. He decided he would need to find families who would give these orphans a home until the orphanage could reopen. So, Anthony prayed:

*"O Lord Jesus, these children are your precious gems, how shall I care for them? You are their Father and we all look to You for help. I cannot send these innocent children back out onto the streets. Please show us a way out as you are a God of miracles. You alone are a God who wipes our tears, and You alone are our Savior. Without Your will not even a hair from our head can fall."*

After praying that prayer he spent the next three days in fasting and prayer along with the 51 orphans. At the end of three days, they still had no answers. Anthony became afraid. He knew that if even one child starved, he would be in grave danger. The enemy simply waited for a chance to twist the truth and turn hard times into a crime so they could jail Anthony forever. So, with great sorrow, he gathered the 51 orphans together. With tears streaming down his cheeks he said, "I will not drive you out onto the streets by force, but those children who want to leave the orphanage can go." The children in unison said, "We will not leave here."

By this time, the people in the local community learned that the children were starving. There was no food and no money to buy food because the ministry accounts had been seized. Miraculously, God worked in the hearts of the village people. Filled with compassion, they decided that they would help care for these orphans. Over the next 11 months, the people in the neighborhood provided the children with food. God blessed these people for opening their hearts and their wallets to these orphans. Friends, our God is not indebted to anyone. The Lord simply offers us an opportunity to do good and thereby become heirs to God's blessings.

The work of Anthony Soren continues to succeed which angers the anti-Christians. They continually threaten to kill him. One day during a prayer meeting, they shot at him. They missed their mark and the bullet struck Anthony's younger brother instead. The bullet entered the boys head just above the eye and pierced the skull, lodging itself in his head. At the hospital a team of doctors operating on him separated his skull to remove the bullet. The doctors gave him a very slim chance of survival. Once the doctors stated that they had little hope for him, everyone else lost hope. But the church prayed for him and by God's grace he survived. Later, a plastic surgeon was able to hide some of the scars he sustained due to his injury. Today this brother is actively and enthusiastically serving God.

We can only imagine the fear this act of violence caused the church. Everyone in this church experienced mental, spiritual and financial pain. It is always discouraging and difficult for Christians to live in the shadow of the fear of violence.

*"Blessed are you, when people insult you, persecute you and falsely say all kinds of evil against you because of Me. Rejoice and be glad because great is your reward in heaven, for in the same way they persecuted the prophets who were before you."*
*Matthew 5:11-12*

When this same group of anti-Christians learned of their failed attempt to kill Anthony, they devised a plot to bomb one of his prayer meetings. Unfortunately, while assembling the detonator for the bomb, it exploded in their faces and three of the four died on the spot. The only survivor, although seriously injured, was arrested.

Two failed attempts made them even more determined to save face with their rebel supporters. Their next move was to falsely accuse Anthony of being a terrorist. They charged him with murder saying that he kills troubled people and then steals their belongings. Anthony was taken to jail and remained there for two months. Both of the Lower

Courts refused his application for bail, but the High Court did grant him bail. The case against him is still open.

There was a major attack against Christians in his area on Christmas Eve, 2007. Many Christians were killed and their homes burned. Anthony and the children in his orphanage had to hide in the forest in the cold of winter among the wild animals in order to escape the persecution. Continuously over the next two years, Christians have been attacked and killed in this area. In spite of these challenges, Anthony Soren is still serving the Lord boldly and with joy. In the midst of these trials, his orphanage has grown by another 20 children!

It is true that "Emmanuel", Jehovah God - the Lord is with us. He is adding to His church and growing it every day in spite of outside appearances. God the Father says,

*"I am with you, I will not leave nor forsake you."*
*Habakkuk13:5*

## Pastor Godda Israel: *Martyr*

 In a small village of Andhra Pradesh, Pastor Godda Israel lived and served God. He and a few other missionaries established 15 churches in their neighborhood. Pastor Godda quickly became a "pain in the side" for the local religious fundamentalists. On January 17, 2007 a few of them approached him and asked if he would accompany them so he could pray for their sick friend. He agreed and was led by these men out of his village.

When the Pastor did not return for several days, the believers went to the police and filed an FIR. But the police refused to record the complaint and would not take any action. Three days later his body was discovered when it floated to the surface of the water. The believers identified the body as that of Pastor Godda Israel. Upon closer examination, it was found that he had been repeatedly stabbed. Even with this information, the police refused to charge anyone with his murder. It was only after Dr. Sajan K. George, President of the Global Council of Indian Christians, intervened that the police filed an FIR.

This servant of God is in heaven today enjoying close communion with the Lord. Pastor Israel is the 14th person martyred while serving God with our ministry. He was only 29 years old when he died.

Please pray for his young widow – Aruna and their
two children.

## Brother Shasikant

 At the India-Nepal border, in the state
of Bihar, Brother Shasikant has been
serving the Lord for many years.
Approximately 140 people attend his
church. He has established a school
and an orphanage as well.

When the religious fundamentalists see any signage
with Christian names on it, one is almost assured of
persecution. A group of these rebels entered Brother
Shasikant's church and beat four believers
mercilessly. They then proceeded to break the
chairs, benches and tables in the church. They
burned the prayer mats, and shaking with anger
threatened, "Leave this village if you do not want to
die or we will kill you". But Brother Shasikant
stood his ground and is still carrying on the Lord's
work in Mission Tolli. During the last summer
holidays, 40 people were baptized, publicly
professing their faith and their decision to live for
God.

**There are hundreds of persecution stories.** I have shared these few for one purpose only. I desire that all who are called to serve the King will remember those who must live with daily persecution. I also ask that you pray for those who persecute us. We are, after all, called to bless our enemies – not curse them – because this is the will of God concerning His people. Perhaps the Lord will give them an opportunity for a heart transformation too. Scripture is clear:

*"Bless them which persecute you: bless, and curse not. Rejoice with them that do rejoice, and weep with them that weep. Be of the same mind one toward another. Mind not high things, but condescend to men of low estate. Be not wise in your own conceits. Recompense to no man evil for evil. Provide things honest in the sight of all men. If it be possible, as much as lieth in you, live peaceably with all men. Dearly beloved, avenge not yourselves, but rather give place unto wrath: for it is written, 'vengeance is Mine; I will repay', saith the Lord. Therefore if thine enemy hunger, feed him; if he thirst, give him drink: for in so doing thou shalt heap coals of fire on his head. Be not overcome of evil, but overcome evil with good."*
*Romans 12:14-21*

Every Bible student signs the Martyr's Oath upon graduation! It is a pledge that our Pioneer Missionaries take before launching out into the mission field. They not only live for the Lord, but vow to die for Him.

## MARTYR'S OATH

1. I stand with the Apostle Paul in stating that "For me to live is Christ and to die is gain."

2. I take a stand to honor the Lord Jesus Christ with my hands and to serve all mankind.

3. I take a stand to honor the Lord Jesus Christ with my feet and spread the Gospel to all the ends of the earth, no matter what the cost.

4.     I take a stand to honor the Lord Jesus Christ with my lips by proclaiming the Good News to all who hear and by edifying the body of Christ.

5. I take a stand to honor the Lord Jesus Christ with my mind as I meditate upon His Word and His promises to me.

6. I give my earthly treasures and all that I possess to follow the way of the cross.

7. I commit to love my family, orphans, widows, lepers, the

wealthy and the poor the way
that Christ loves the Church.

8. I surrender my will and life to
His will and life.

9. I commit to the service of the
Lord by being a good steward
of my time.

10.    I surrender this body on
earth to the perfect will of
Jesus and should my blood be

spilled, may it bring forth a
mighty harvest of souls.

11.     I pledge allegiance to the
Lamb. I will seek to honor
His commands; I am not
ashamed of the Gospel of
Christ for it is the power of
God unto salvation to everyone
who believes.

12.     Lord Jesus, Thy
Kingdom come; Thy will be

*done on earth as it is in heaven.*

13.     *I love my nation and my fellow citizens and I claim my nation for Christ.*

***I have read this pledge and understand it completely. Being of sound mind and body, I do solemnly declare this martyr's pledge without any persuasion or enticement.***

**I, _____,
from_____(place of birth)**

**Do hereby make the following covenant on this
_____day of _____in the year\_\_\_\_.**

### Truth Alone Triumphs
***From: Satyameva Jayate***

Show of power is a mark of ungodliness.

Sign of tolerance is the soul of religion.
Whoever picks up a weapon to defend his religion;
is showing forth the weakness of the faith.
Some devotees take refuge in religion
While some ungodly take the religion under their
refuge.
But, whoever takes refuge in the true God,
embraces the grief-stricken to his bosom.
Because the living God does not look for religious
conversion; rather He desires the transformation of
the hearts. And a true religion does not require
weapon; but it requires true love. Not authority over
others; but a denying of the self.

Hopegivers International would like to
hear from you!
If you liked this book, please introduce it
to others.

If you want to know more about Hopegivers
International and its ministries,
please visit our website at:

## www.hopegivers.org

## Write us:
Hopegivers International
P. O. Box 8808
Columbus, Georgia 31908
info@hopegivers.org

**Your friend and co-worker**
*Bishop Dr. Samuel Thomas*

*"Don't count your days, make your days count!"*

CPSIA information can be obtained at www.ICGtesting.com
Printed in the USA
LVIW01n1358110915
453560LV00002B/2